FRANK SULLIVAN
AT HIS BEST

Frank Sullivan

with a new Introduction by
Herb Galewitz

DOVER PUBLICATIONS, INC.
Mineola, New York

Bibliographical Note

This Dover edition, first published in 1996, is new selection of 42 essays taken from three anthologies first published by Little, Brown and Company, Boston: *A Pearl in Every Oyster* (1938), *A Rock in Every Snowball* (1946) and *The Night the Old Nostalgia Burned Down* (1948). A new introduction has been written by Herb Galewitz, for whose help the publisher is most grateful.

Library of Congress Cataloging-in-Publication Data

Sullivan, Frank, 1892–1976.
    Frank Sullivan at his best / Frank Sullivan.
        p.   cm.
    ISBN 0-486-29435-8 (pbk)
    1. American essays.   I. Title.
PS3537.U47A6   1996
814'.52—dc20   96-21708
                                                                                   CIP

Manufactured in the United States of America
Dover Publications, Inc., 31 East 2nd Street, Mineola, N.Y. 11501

Introduction to the Dover Edition

by
Herb Galewitz

F RANK SULLIVAN (1892–1976) was among that heady group of humorists that seemed to burst on the New York literary scene during the 1920's. His contemporaries and friends included F.P.A., Robert Benchley, Dorothy Parker, Marc Connelly, Heywood Broun, George S. Kaufman, Donald Ogden Stewart and Corey Ford, to name a glittering few. The only reason why Sullivan did not join them at the Algonquin Round Table is that his newspaper chores kept him busy until 11 P.M. and he didn't do "lunch."

However, after work, the convivial Sullivan would head for the popular speakeasys — Tony Soma's, Dan Moriarity's and Bleeck's — where he would more than likely run into Benchley, Parker or Thurber, all equally serious imbibers. Or else he might join in an all-night poker game, another passion shared by many of the Algonquins. The nocturnal habit was to remain with Sullivan for most of his life.

Critics have called Sullivan "a gentle humorist and spoofer." But it was a gentleness that had a feather tickler attached to it, keeping the reader chuckling, giggling and generally appreciative of the word play, the mock seriousness, the stream-of-consciousness patter that could have been in the script of an early Marx Brothers movie — such as the pronouncements of his creation Mr. Arbuthnot, The Cliché Expert, with a penchant for using the well-worn phrase.

The silly antics of celebrities were fair game, along with the vicissitudes of living in New York — street obstructions due to a never-ending cycle of building and tearing down structures, the street cacophony that clashes with the attempts at sleep, the shrill, un-fathomable cries of street urchins that could rattle the nerves of an at-home writer.

He could spoof various crazes with his own inventions, out-footnote literary Van Wyck Brooks, or witness nostalgia through the rose-colored glasses of exaggeration.

What was Frank Sullivan really like? In appearance, he was said to resemble a turn-of-the-century high-school principal, favoring slightly outdated conservative clothes on his pudgy frame while peering through pince-nez eyeglasses. Let Mr. Sullivan tell you about his background as related in *Vogue* magazine some years ago —

> Francis John Sullivan is that *rara avis*, a native of Saratoga Springs, where he was born in 1892, the son of Lotta Crabtree and Harold W. Ross. He made his first appearance on the stage two months later playing Fleance to Mme. Modjeska's Lady Macbeth. A promising stage career was terminated soon afterward when, during a performance at Harmanus Bleeker Hall in Albany, Mrs. Modjeska dropped the budding Fleance on his head. The next day Sullivan became a humorist and startled the literary world with a brilliant novel of one man's love for the woman he loves, "What Makes Martin Chuzzlewit Run?" ("Could not put it down" — Hamilton Wright Mabie. "Held me from start to finish" — Brander Matthews. "Perfectly corking but lacks an index" — James Gibbons Huneker.)
>
> Frank is five feet six inches high and about the same across and sleeps in the raw. His pupils dilate normally but his mainspring needs tightening. He spent the summer of 1910 pasting labels on bottles of Saratoga water. We shall later see how this affected the campaign of 1912. . . .

The real Frank Sullivan was born and raised in Saratoga Springs, graduated with a degree from Cornell in 1914, worked on a newspaper in his hometown, served in the U.S. Army during World

War I, and after the war moved to New York for work on several newspapers before being hired by Herbert Bayard Swope for the *World*. His journalism career almost came to an end when, in a celebrated faux pax, Sullivan wrote a page-one obituary for a prominent New York society woman who unfortunately (for him) turned out to be alive. He was then assigned to cover more mundane affairs such as "demonstrations of kiss-proof lipsticks."

1925 was the turning point in Sullivan's career. Swope asked him to substitute for the popular and influential F.P.A., who was going on vacation, and write his column; while *The New Yorker* magazine, in its first year of existence, accepted three Sullivan pieces for publication. His association with *The New Yorker* lasted until 1974, when the last of the annual Christmas poems, "Greetings, Friends," was published. When the New York *World* folded in 1931, Sullivan went on to a free-lance career as a frequent contributor to *The Saturday Evening Post, Good Housekeeping, Town & Country* and, of course, *The New Yorker*. During World War II, he wrote a column for the short-lived newspaper *PM*.

After twenty years of New York living, Sullivan returned to his beloved Saratoga Springs, where he remained for the rest of his bachelor life writing his delightful pieces, carrying on an extensive correspondence with his many friends, famous and otherwise, and greeting them on visits to his modest home.

8, 23, 48, 77, 85, 106, 141
59-65

Contents

Street Cries of New York

THE STREET CRIES of great cities have always been for me one of the most fascinating of studies. When traveling, I continually keep my ear to the ground for them, except when I am in a hurry or my back hurts. I daresay I could go blindfolded into any one of fifty cities scattered over the globe and tell you offhand where we were, merely by listening to the street cries.

In the richness and variety of its cries, New York is surpassed by no city; not by London, and not even by Benares at howdah-dusting time. The most favorable period for studying New York street cries is from about April 1st until the latter part of August. At the former date, the buyers of cash clothes and the vendors of bananas, geraniums, tulips, and ganeezles emerge from their hibernation and from then until well into August are to be heard constantly, from five in the morning until well past sundown. But at the end of August, when the hot weather has had its effect on the nerves of the city dwellers, the so-called Period of Mayhem starts. People begin to shy eggs, electric-light bulbs, and stone bookends at the street criers. A great many of them are maimed as a result and an equal number become panicky and stampede, so that from about the third Tuesday in August the cries begin to wane until they reach the ebb in mid-January.

In the spring, the tulip-vendors are almost invariably the first to appear on the streets with their wares. Their cry may be rendered as follows: "Ah wo-o-o hah! Ah wo-o-o hah!" Roughly translated, this means "Tulips for sale. Nice fresh tulips for sale." With their picturesque costumes of coat, cap, pants, vest, and shoes, the tulip-vendors are as real a harbinger of spring as the crocus or the robin.

Next to appear are the geranium-vendors, and when we see their carts, brilliant splotches of scarlet, pink, and green, we know indeed that spring is here. The cry of the geranium-sellers is one of the most arresting and ancient of street cries, and goes like this: "Ow wow ho-o-o! Ow wow ho-o-o!" It means "Geraniums!" Owing to the similarity in the respective costumes of the tulip- and geranium-vendors, many street-cry authorities claim that the geranium-vendors are nothing more than tulip-vendors selling geraniums instead of tulips, but we need not here concern ourselves with such fine points of issue.

"Ripa da banan'!"—When we hear this cry in New York, rendered usually in the majestic bellow that results from the action of Mediterranean sun and salt air on the larynx of the native Calabrian, we know indeed that spring is here. It is the cry of the vendor of the banana. Banana-vendors usually hail from Calabria. Translated roughly, the cry means "Nisa fresha banan' for sale. Who will buy my nisa fresha banan' for sale?"

"Bly whamp clew!"—This is the cry of the old-clothes solicitor and can be translated as "Buy cash cloe!" It is not dissimilar to the cry of the Paris delphinium-sellers: "Burrump badoo! Barrump badoo!"

"Ganee-e-e-zle!"—One of the most interesting of the New York street cries. Part of its charm is due to its mystery—at least it is for me, because I have never been able to find out what it means. I have repeatedly tried to collar a crier of "Ganee-e-e-zle!" but without success. He seems to be the most evanescent of all the vendors, and no matter how swiftly I chase down to the street on hearing this cry, I have never been able to find anything that could be identified as a ganeezle-crier. My researches were confined to the block in which I live—and it would be interesting to know if "Ganee-e-e-zle!" is a purely local cry or common to the entire city. It has been suggested by a fellow-connoisseur of street cries, Miss Patricia Collinge, that the crier of "Ganee-e-e-zle!" sells ganeezles, and this seems a reasonable hypothesis, except that Dr. Collinge has not been able to establish what a ganeezle is. Any information on this point would be appreciated.

Q: Any other kind of people get murdered?

A: Yes, elderly spinsters living alone and believed to have large sums of money hidden about the house. In such cases, robbery is the motive, police believe.

Q: Where does a murder take place?

A: In a sparsely settled region, or section of town. That is, if it takes place out of doors. If indoors, it usually takes place in a love nest, a water-front dive, a gangster hideout, or a sumptuously furnished apartment.

Q: With what are people usually murdered?

A: Some blunt instrument was used in the commission of the crime, police aver.

Q: Who finds the body?

A: Small boys playing in a vacant lot come upon the still form, huddled in a heap. They notify the police.

Q: When?

A: Immediately.

Q: What happens then?

A: A crowd gathers.

Q: What kind of crowd?

A: A crowd of morbid curiosity-seekers who stand riveted in horror at the gruesome sight.

Q: What then?

A: Then the coroner arrives.

Q: What does he do?

A: He performs his grim task. He pronounces the man dead.

Q: What does an autopsy do?

A: An autopsy reveals.

Q: What do the police suspect?

A: Foul play.

Q: What do the neighbors do?

A: They report that they heard a shot during the night but thought nothing of it, believing it to be the backfire of an automobile.

Q: What is there no sign of after the crime?

A: There is no sign of a weapon.

Q: What does a murder do to the police?

A: It baffles them.

Q: What do they do in an effort to become less baffled?

A: They comb the city, spread a police dragnet, search all known haunts of underworld characters, and try to find a clue.

Q: What kind of clue?

A: A promising clue.

Q: What happens then?

A: The police expect a break in the case any moment. They announce that a solution of the murder will be arrived at within twenty-four hours. Or forty-eight hours.

Q: Never twenty-three hours, or forty-seven?

A: Oh, no, Judge. That would be decidedly irregular. A cliché expert using such a term would risk severe censure and possible ostracism by his colleagues.

Q: What happens to the victim just before the crime?

A: He is last seen alive.

Q: Ever cover a bank robbery, or pay-roll holdup, Mr. Arbuthnot?

A: Loads of 'em.

Q: Good. Who commit holdups?

A: A band of masked bandits.

Q: What do their guns do?

A: They bark.

Q: After the holdup the bandits escape, of course.

A: Oh, no. Bandits never escape. They *make good* their escape.

Q: How?

A: Oh, Mr. McReynolds, surely you know the answer to that one. Everybody does.

Q: It is a question of getting it on the record, if you don't mind. Will you answer the question, please?

A: Well, in a high-powered car. How else? A high-powered car that drew up to the curb before the holdup, and had been waiting there, with motor running.

Q: What always happens to one of the bandits?

A: One of the bandits is believed to have been wounded in the getaway.

Q: What kind of car is used in gang killings?

A: A death car.

Q: Who flee?

A: The assailants flee.

Q: What kind of accomplices do criminals have?

A: Only one kind—alleged.

Q: What kind of intruders break into houses?

A: Unknown intruders who were seen lurking in the vicinity shortly before the crime.

Q: What does tragedy do?

A: Tragedy stalks.

Q: What are suspects under?

A: Under police surveillance.

Q: Now then, Mr. Arbuthnot, if the culprits do not escape—I mean, do not make good their escape—it is logical, is it not, to assume that they are caught?

A: Oh, not caught. They are apprehended. Or, even better, taken into custody. Never say caught when you can say apprehended or taken into custody.

Q: After they are taken into custody, what is it they do about their innocence?

A: They protest their innocence.

Q: And they deny—?

A: All knowledge of the crime.

Q: Then what happens to them?

A: They are grilled.

Q: You mean the police attempt to get a confession from them?

A: Judge, the police never *get* a confession. They *wring* it.

Q: What then?

A: Then comes the trial.

Q: Describe the trial, please.

A: The trial is an ordeal, for which the accused must steel himself.

Q: Why?

A: Because he knows the district attorney is going to subject him to a gruelling cross-examination.

Q: Which district attorney?

A: The brilliant young district attorney.

Q: With the—?

A: With the bright political future.

Q: What does the prisoner show?

A: No sign of emotion.

Q: How does he get to the stand?

A: He shuffles to the stand.

Q: If the prisoner at the bar is a young woman, what is it she cries so often during the trial?

A: You mean " 'It's a lie!' she cried, sobbing"?

Q: That's it. What does the judge do?

A: He threatens to clear the courtroom.

Q: How is the verdict greeted?

A: The verdict is greeted with cheers.

Q: If the prisoner does not get a verdict that is greeted with cheers, what is it he has to pay?

A: His debt to society.

Q: Thank you, Mr. Arbuthnot. You have been a great help. You may step down.

A: The pleasure's all mine, Judge. Call on me any time.

Pencil-Chewing

THE PENCIL-CHEWERS constitute one class of unfortunates whose misery science has done nothing to relieve. These poor creatures cannot see a pencil lying about loose without being seized by a craving to make a meal of it. They are on the increase, and something ought to be done, not only for their sakes but in the interest of forest conservation. With the Japanese beetle destroying the elms and the Christmas-tree brokers hacking away at the firs, the timber situation in the United States is bad enough without having people eating cedar unnecessarily.

You see traces of the pencil-chewers everywhere. I am writing this very protest in a fit of pique because a moment ago I picked up a chewed pencil. It looked as though it had been worried by a neurotic beaver. It had been gnawed with an avidity that bordered on the dendrophilic. Most pencil-eaters content themselves with nibbling at the unsharpened end of the pencil, then passing on to other pencils, like tapirs ravishing buds in a jungle. But this pencil has been permanently crippled.

Obviously, the addict who wrought this havoc was in an advanced stage of the habit, and probably incurable. In such a case the only humane thing to do is to feed the poor creature all the pencils he can eat, so that he may succumb to lead and cedar poisoning as quickly as possible, to find peace in a perhaps pencilless Beyond.

It has never ceased to be a source of wonderment to me why a man should prefer to chew pencils when food that is far more wholesome and filling can be procured at a trifling cost. No pencil-chewer can tell me he cannot afford better food. A bowl of good, nourishing soup can be had anywhere for the price of a soft lead pencil, and contains more calories. Anyhow, persons who are really hungry are rarely pencil-chewers. The latter are recruited from the better-fed but more hysterical upper classes. They claim that chewing on a pencil helps them to think. There was a case here in New York last fall of a prominent American novelist who, during the writing of one of these eleven-hundred-page novels that are all the rage now, swallowed so much cedar that he had to go to the hospital shortly before Christmas to be operated on, and they removed enough timber from him to supply the Yule log for the Christmas celebration at the hospital. He sent the hospital a bill for three dollars for wood and supplies.

Sometimes pencil-chewers can go for years and years without giving any outward indications of the habit, such as sprouting cedar twigs or having pine knots appear on their elbows, but eventually it gets them. An addict I heard of gnawed pencils for thirty years without seeming to suffer any ill effects, until one day, to everybody's surprise, he suddenly screamed that he was a pencil and tried to stick his head into the office pencil-sharpener. Rescued from the sharpener, he kept trying to nestle in his stenographer's ear. He recovered eventually, but not until he had gone about for a long time begging his friends to whittle him.

What can we do to help the pencil-gnawer? It is no use suggesting a Stop Selling These campaign to limit the sale of pencils to proved non-chewers. This would only increase pencil-chewing by making it more alluring.

It might be possible to help the chewer by diverting his attention to more succulent tidbits. Let him make it a rule never to approach a pencil when hungry; never to use a pencil on an empty stomach. That will lessen the urge to eat the pencil. Then, while using a pencil, let the addict arrange to have a supply of food close at hand. The food ought to be tempting, so as to outweigh the charms of the pencil—a tasty custard, a bonbon, a spiced cookie, or a forkful of finnan haddie. Then, whenever he feels the urge to take a bite of the pencil, he can reach for one of the more orthodox dainties.

Or we can attack the problem from another angle. We can make it impossible for the addict to chew the pencil by making a pencil that is impossible to chew. The trouble with present pencils is that they are made of soft woods, easy to chew. The unchewable pencil would be made of teak, which is one of the hardest woods in the world, comes from Ceylon and has never been successfully gnawed. A teak pencil would be apt to thwart the efforts of the most determined pencil-nibbler, and save him from himself. Care should be taken, however, lest the nibbler, in a fit of rage at finding himself baffled, swallow the pencil entire.

In the last analysis, the most thorough method of dealing with the problem of pencil-chewing is through education. Pencil-chewers become pencil-chewers because chewing pencils helps them to think. Therefore, it is the task of those who wish to help them to train them in the use of other, and less harmful, aids to thought.

There are many such aids. Lots of thinkers who never touch a pencil get excellent results by tearing their hair and rolling their eyes frantically, as a stimulant to the production of creative work. This, however, does not mean that a thinker who is bald, or who cannot roll his eyes, or both, must resort to chewing pencils. Not at all. There are still other aids to thought.

Biting the lower lip, for instance, is one of the best. Many of our foremost pundits do their most effective thinking while biting the lower lip. This method accomplishes fully as much to help speed the thought process as biting on a lead pencil, and is neater and not nearly so dangerous. Neater, because thinkers cannot leave old bitten lips around on desks for other thinkers to pick up; less dangerous, because the lower lip can stand a good deal of biting without suffering any material damage. If occasionally, in the course of some particularly brilliant job of thinking, a wiseacre absent-mindedly nips off a portion of his lip, the damage is soon remedied by Mother Nature, or by surgery.

If you are a bald thinker, and you cannot or do not care to roll your eyes, and are averse to biting the lower lip, you can groan or mumble, or wring the hands, as an aid to creative output. Personally, I am a groaner and an eye-roller, with intervals of mumbling and wringing the hands. I also chew a pencil occasionally, but in moderation. All during this article, for instance, I have been mumbling and uttering low screams, rolling the right eye appealingly toward heaven from time to time. Perhaps you have, too.

Gentlemen Should Smell
Pretty, Too

THE GIRLS OF today float through life in clouds of the most divine perfumes, leaving groggy but contented males strewn along the battlefield right and left, slap-happy victims of this fragrant form of gas warfare. This is the golden age of scentology. I venture the statement that ladies have never been so aromatic as they are today. Men, alas, smell about as they always have.

Not only are modern perfumes rare and wonderful, but they have wonderful names. What amounts to a new romantic school of literature has come into being especially to celebrate them. Some of the most gifted poets and word slingers in this land of the free twang their lyres in praise of the marvelous new attars.

As a male confined by a silly taboo to the use of nothing more redolent than bay rum, I read with envy and awe the descriptions of the costly lotions that ladies douse themselves with. For instance, regarding an essence with the pleasantly ominous name of *Cobra*, I read that "the woman who wears *Cobra* stands out alone in her beauty like some new divine instrument soloing to the gods."

On the bottle of hair tonic I use it says, "Removes dandruff, helps check excessive falling hair, relieves itching scalp, keeps the hair in place, giving a well-groomed but not greasy appearance."

That's the build-up I get when I tidy myself up. That's the build-up the average American male gets. I envy that little girl who is going to

solo to the gods after she dabs *Cobra* behind her ears. I'd sort of like
to be a divine instrument myself, standing out alone in my beauty.
But the best I can look forward to is that my hair will stay in place
and I won't be greasy. Well, I suppose that is something; but whatever it is, it is not poetry. Yet lots of us American men have souls for
beauty, just like Charles Boyer, if the manufacturers of men's toilet
preparations only knew it. We are the victims of a hang-over from
the rigorous pioneer days of our country, when men did not have
time to smell pretty. If Dan Boone had an itching scalp, there was
always a redskin around with a tomahawk to relieve it for him—or
him of it.

Now, that is a wonderful boost in morale that the *Cobra* people
gave a girl. She comes home all in, after a tough day on the assem-
bly line. She does not feel like a divine instrument. Her powers to
bewitch and sparkle are functioning on one cylinder. Her *amour-
propre* is full of clinkers. She feels not unlike Grandma in *Tobacco
Road*. Up steps her perfume. It does not give her any cold comfort
of telling her that her hair won't fall out excessively. No lugubrious,
negative compliments. Friend in need that it is, it takes the stand
such a friend would take: it tells her she is a divine instrument and
that she is going to solo to the gods, standing out alone in her beauty.
Against a girl thus bolstered and confident, what chance has a man
got whose only assurance is that his hair is in place?

Maybe the girl is partial to another perfume. It makes no difference. They all stand ready to buck her up. Not a one is a Job's com-
forter. If she is fond of a scent called Orloff's *Attar of Petals*, she
will learn that it will "set the seal of perfection on [her] loveliness
and enthrall the senses with the pulse-quickening fragrance of sun-
kissed blossoms." If she likes *Écarlate de Suzy*, she is advised that
"its dry, winy sparkle seems to loosen some spring in the man of
taut nerves and dark moods." If she favors a charmingly named attar called *Breathless*, she is told that it is "made for those moments
when your pulse quickens—when you live an eternity—and the
world is yours."

If the brushless shaving cream I use were to tell me that it was
about to set the seal of perfection on my loveliness, or loosen my
springs with its dry winy sparkle, or quicken my pulse and hand me
the world, why, I think I'd holler "Whoop-de-do! Burn my clothes!",
dive out the window and chase every lady in my neighborhood

right up into the Adirondack Mountains, a distance of thirty miles from my doorstep. But on my jar of shaving cream it says, "Important—Keep tightly closed after using. Net wt. 15¼ oz."

Keep tightly closed after shaving, eh? Well, I'm getting a little tired of that kind of repression. I would like to blossom after shaving. I, and a great many other frustrated macaronis, would like to have access to a shaving cream that would "unlock our hearts and provide white magic for moments of unfettered joy." (That's what the perfume called *Escape* promises for the ladies who dab it behind their ears.) "Net weight, 15¼ oz.!" They wouldn't even throw in that extra ¾ of an oz. and call it a pound!

It's witch hazel for the men; witch hazel in all its stark, stinging astringency. For the girls it is the above lovely essences and hosts of others, with palpitating, provocative names like *Heartbeat, Danger, Risqué, Nuit d'Amour, Poetic Dream, Toujours ou Jamais, Chichi, Intoxication, Toujours Fidèle, Moment Suprême, Startling, Mais Oui, Enchantment, White Flame, Désir du Coeur, Mon Ami* and *Frolic*.

Quite a few of the perfumes harp symbolically on the warfare motif: Solon Palmer, one of the real humdingers among American *parfumeurs*, dedicates *Fragrance of Victory* "to the cadence of the drumbeat, to the quickening pulse of American womanhood on the march to Victory!" Run for the hills, boys, the girls have crossed the Delaware! Then there are perfumes called *Courage, Surrender* and *Secret Weapon for a Lady*. Secret, eh? What's secret about a weapon that any foe with his olfactory nerve in good working order can detect at a distance of a block? And what kind of warfare is it where a lacy white handkerchief serves as a weapon of attack instead of a flag of truce?

I have often wondered how they name the perfumes. I know, of course, that when the American Academy of Pullman Nomenclature holds its annual meeting for the purpose of naming the Pullman cars for the ensuing fiscal year, they simply take a flower-seed catalogue, a list of noted American battles, a roster of two hundred American cities and some names of Hollywood pretties, let them come to a boil and then strain off the Pullman-car names as they bubble to the surface. I know that botanists seeking to name new plants, and doctors looking for names for new diseases, take a copy of Caesar's *Commentaries* jettisoned by some maddened high-school student and stick a pin at random into any word. If it has more than four syllables their plant, or disease, is named.

To date I have not been able to wheedle any *parfumeur* into betraying the secret of perfume nomenclature. However, I think I can make a shrewd guess as to what happens. When they want to name a new perfume, all the prominent distillers of pretty smells assemble in a luxurious salon lined with pink satin and summon one of the staff poets from the ivory tower where he lives in sybaritic thralldom. They give him a swig of the perfume about to be named. A mere thimbleful, or about forty dollars' worth, suffices. Under its potent spell the poet lapses into a trance and pretty soon begins to mutter lovely, lush names and phrases such as "Secret weapon for a lady. . . Intoxicating as a kiss . . . Intriguing as a suppressed look . . . Taboo . . . Fragrance for the woman beloved," and so on.

Then whoever has been appointed recording secretary for the séance eagerly jots down everything the drugged bard utters. Then they take their pick.

It is very possible that this is what happens. After all, Coleridge wrote "Kubla Khan" in a dream, and "Kubla Khan" is a poem that ranks with some of the finest rhapsodies that have been written about modern perfumes. More than that, I have seen with my own eyes how the consumption of vegetable essences can speed up the creative effort. I knew a top sergeant in the last war who went AWOL once and returned to camp four days later in a blitzed condition of mind and body. He went directly to the mess hall and drank a large bottle of lemon extract, raw. He then gave a loud cry and went into a coma. It took four men to bear him to the guardhouse, and on the way there he extemporized, in his trance, some of the most picturesque free verse that had been heard in the United States Army since the Battle of Bunker Hill. It was lovely, purple free verse, but none of it could have been used to apostrophize ladies' perfumes.

If my shaving lotion, instead of being called what it is called, were renamed something like *Le Killer Diller*, or *Jamais Noisome*, or *Embrassez-moi, Toots!* and if instead of being announced as an excellent after-shave lotion also good as a body rubdown, it were described as "the lotion that makes a man's jowl as exciting as a velvet poem; the magic tonsoriate that will bewitch your favorite Hazel; the tonic that will make a man stand out alone in his virile beauty"—why, if I got a build-up like that from my lotion, I'd be playing quarterback on every conga line in café society from the club El Gyppo to the club El Stucko, instead of lying down for an hour after dinner with the evening paper over my face.

Arise, gentlemen! To arms, nonfragrant papas! Muss up your hair. Leave the top of your shaving-cream jar untightened. Let us swear not to shave until we get some color into our drab toiletries. Let us storm the rose-covered bowers of the poets laureate of perfumery and make them rewrite the blurbs for our hair tonics and shaving creams, and pretty them up. Let us have fancy monikers to *our* lotions, that will make us feel like conquering heroes out-Granting Cary and out-Coopering Gary.

Lawyers' Lingo

AFTER A FEW hundred of the more pressing post-war problems have been solved, it might not be a bad idea to launch a movement to put the legal profession on Basic English. Even if it could be got back to just plain English that would be so much velvet. Legal English needs a thorough overhauling. It needs to have an expert go through it, rake the underbrush of last year's adjectives and other superfluous verbiage and burn them.

Some time ago, the Judge invited Attorney Broderick, the Peck's Bad Boy of the Lonergan trial, into the woodshed, or courtroom, for a conference about Broderick's antics during the part of the trial Judge Freschi directed. This is what went on, according to the account in the *Times*.

Judge Freschi said that on March 3, "while the Court was transacting its business," Mr. Broderick gave with "a most violent, vociferous outburst of unjustifiable and irrelevant vituperation, insinuation, abuse, false statements, shouting, table-pounding and an address to the jury. . . ."

The Judge meant that Broderick raised hell in court.

He continued:—

"Not only were the language, words and acts contemptuous, but the circumstances, tone, look, manner and emphasis, all collectively, afforded the Court an opportunity to observe the character of your contemptuous, insolent manner toward him."

What was Mr. Broderick's reply to this? Did he seize a marvelous opportunity to say just: "Not guilty"? Not on your life. Had he done so he would have been false to every polysyllabic tradition of the gabbiest profession in the world and would have earned for himself the scorn, censure, disapproval, disesteem, ostracism, disparagement, condemnation, strictures and criticism of his colleagues.

What he said was:—

"I deny vigorously, but without vehemence, that I had willfully or deliberately intended to be contumacious, contemptuous, insolent, disorderly or derogatory of the authority, integrity or dignity of the Court or Judge."

He meant he didn't do it. Nevertheless, the Judge sentenced him to thirty days in the clink, keep, donjon, hoosegow, stir, cooler, bastille, bride, panopticon, pen, bilboes or calaboose.

Why do lawyers talk like that? It's one thing to impress a client, but why do they like to talk to *each other* like that? The more words a lawyer can get into a brief, and the longer the words are, the more delighted he is. A lawyer hates a one-syllable word as the devil hates holy water.

We wish we were a novelist and could write novels as lawyers write their briefs and then have the good fortune to find an editor who would pay us ten cents a word. Holy Jumping Jiminy, we, the party of the first part, would be richer, i.e. and to wit, we'd have a larger income, reward, remuneration, quittance, compensation, requital, perquisite, allowance, salary, stipend, wage, payment, emolument, batta, premium, fee, honorarium or dasturi, than the whole, entire, complete or unabridged firm of Root, Clark, Buckner, Davis, Polk, Wardwell, Untermyer, Driscoll, Malevinsky and O'Brien.

The Cliché Expert Testifies
on the Atom

Q: MR. ARBUTHNOT, you're the very man I want to see. I've been longing to examine you on atomic energy.

A: Well, my boy, you've come to the right party. I believe I can say that I know all the clichés on the subject.

Q: How can you say that?

A: Without fear of successful contradiction.

Q: I'm glad to hear it. I suspected you would be making a study of the atomic cliché.

A: A study! Why I've been doing nothing since V-J Day but listen to the experts explain atomic energy and the bomb on the air, or editorialize about them in the newspapers. Indeed I *am* the cliché expert of the atom. You realize of course what the dropping of that test bomb in the stillness of the New Mexico night did.

Q: What did it do?

A: It ushered in the atomic age, that's what it did. You know what kind of discovery this is?

Q: What kind?

A: A tremendous scientific discovery.

Q: Could the atomic age have arrived by means of any other verb than "usher"?

A: No. "Usher" has the priority.

Q: Mr. Arbuthnot, what will never be the same?

A: The world.

Q: Are you pleased?

A: I don't know. The splitting of the atom could prove a boon to mankind. It could pave the way for a bright new world. On the other hand it may spell the doom of civilization as we know it.

Q: You mean that it has—

A: Vast possibilities for good or evil.

Q: At any rate, Mr. Arbuthnot, as long as the bomb had to be discovered, I'm glad we got it first.

A: If you don't mind, I will be the one to recite the clichés here. You asked me to, you know.

Q: I'm sorry.

A: Quite all right. I shudder to think.

Q: What?

A: Of what might have happened if Germany or Japan had got the bomb first.

Q: What kind of race was it between the Allied and German scientists?

A: A close race.

Q: What pressed?

A: Time pressed.

Q: With what kind of energy did the scientists work in their race to get the bomb?

A: Feverish energy. Had the war lasted another six months the Germans might have had the bomb. It boggles.

Q: What boggles?

A: This tremendous scientific discovery boggles the imagination. Also stirs same.

Q: Where do we stand, Mr. Arbuthnot?

A: At the threshold of a new era.

Q: And humanity is where?

A: At the crossroads. Will civilization survive? Harness.

Q: Harness, Mr. Arbuthnot? What about it?

A: Harness and unleash. You had better learn to use those two words, my boy, if you expect to talk about the atom, or write about it, either. They are two words very frequently used. With pea, of course.

Q: Why pea?

A: Oh, everything is in terms of the pea. You know how much U–235 it would take to drive a car to the moon and back?

Q: No, sir. How much?

A: A lump the size of a pea. Know how much U–235 it would take to ring your electric doorbell for twenty million years?

Q: How much, God forbid?

A: A lump the size of a pea. Know how much it would take to lift the Empire State Building twelve miles into the air?

Q: I wish you would let the Empire State Building alone, Mr. Arbuthnot. It is all right where it is.

A: Sorry. It must be lifted twelve miles into the air. Otherwise, do you know who would not be able to understand the practical application, or meaning, of atomic energy?

Q: No. Who?

A: The average layman.

Q: I see. Well, in that case, up she goes. I gather that a lump the size of a pea would do it.

A: Exactly.

Q: You wouldn't settle for a lump the size of a radish, or a bean?

A: Sorry. The pea is the accepted vegetable in these explanations. Do you know what the atomic energy in the lobe of your left ear could do?

Q: What?

A: If harnessed, it could propel a B–29 from Tokyo to San Francisco.

Q: It *could!*

A: Do you know that the energy in every breath you take could send the Twentieth Century Limited from New York to Chicago?

Q: Mercy on us, Mr. Arbuthnot!

A: And the atomic energy in your thumbnail could, if unleashed, destroy a city twice the size of three Seattles. Likewise, the energy in your . . .

Q: For God's sake, stop, Mr. Arbuthnot! You make me feel like a menace to world security in dire need of control by international authority in the interests of world peace. Kindly leave off explaining atomic energy to me in terms so simple a layman can understand. Explain it to me in scientific terms, and the more abstruse the better.

A: Well, listen carefully and I'll give you a highly technical explanation. In the first place the existence of the atom was only suspected. Then Einstein . . . equation . . . nucleus . . . electron . . . bombard . . . proton . . . deuteron . . . radioactive . . . neutron . . . atomic weight . . . beta rays . . . matter . . . split . . . chain reaction . . . gamma rays . . . alpha particles . . . Mme. Curie . . . break down . . . energy . . . end products . . . control . . . impact . . . uranium . . . Dr. Niels Bohr . . . barium . . . orbit . . . Dr. Lise Meitner . . . knowledge pooled . . . Dr. Enrico Fermi . . . military possibilities . . . Dr. Vannevar Bush . . . U–235 . . . isotopes . . . U–238 . . . autocatalytic . . . heavy water . . . New Mexico . . . mushroom-shaped cloud . . . awesome sight . . . fission . . . William L. Laurence . . . and there you had a weapon potentially destructive beyond the wildest nightmares of science. Do I make myself clear?

Q: Perfectly. Now, Mr. Arbuthnot, what is nuclear energy the greatest discovery since?

A: It is the greatest discovery since the discovery of fire. You will find that "Promethean" is the correct adjective to use here.

Q: What does this tremendous scientific discovery do to large armies?

A: It spells the doom of large armies. It also spells the doom of large navies. Likewise, it spells the doom of large air forces. Similarly, as I mentioned earlier, it may spell the doom of civilization. I doubt if so many dooms have been spelled by anything since the phrase was first coined.

Q: When was that, sir?

A: I should imagine at the time gunpowder spelled the doom of the bow and arrow.

Q: What is the atomic bomb a menace to?

A: World order, world peace, and world security.

Q: What must be done to it?

A: It must be controlled by an international authority. The San Francisco Charter must be revised to fit the Atomic Age.

Q: What does the bomb make essential?

A: It makes world unity essential. It makes an international league for peace essential if the world is not to be plunged into a third war which will destroy civilization.

Q: In short, its use must be—

A: Banned.

Q: What kind of plaything is the bomb?

A: A dangerous plaything. A dangerous toy.

Q: What kind of boomerang is it?

A: A potential boomerang.

Q: What else is it?

A: It is the greatest challenge mankind has yet faced. It is also the greatest destructive force in history. It has revolutionary possibilities and enormous significance and its discovery caused international repercussions.

Q: What does the splitting of the atom unleash?

A: The hidden forces of the universe. Vast.

Q: Vast?

A: That's another word you'd better keep at hand if you expect to talk or write about this tremendous scientific discovery. Vast energy, you know. Vast possibilities. Vast implications. Vast prospects; it opens them.

Q: I see. What cannot grasp the full significance of the tremendous scientific discovery?

A: The human mind.

Q: Whose stone is it?

A: The philosopher's stone.

Q: Whose dream?

A: The alchemist's dream.

Q: And whose monster?

A: Frankenstein's monster.

Q: What does it transcend?

A: It transcends the wildest imaginings of Jules Verne.

Q: And of who else?

A: H. G. Wells.

Q: The fantastic prophecies of these gentlemen have become what?

A: Stern reality.

Q: What does it make seem tame?

A: The adventures of Superman and Flash Gordon.

Q: Very good, Mr. Arbuthnot. Now, then, in addition to ushering in the Atomic Age, what else does this T.S.D. do?

A: It brightens the prospect for the abolition of war but increases the possibility of another war. It adds to the store of human knowledge. It unlocks the door to the mysteries of the universe. It

makes flights into interstellar space a possibility. It endangers our
security and makes future aggression a temptation.

Q: What has it done to warfare?

A: It has revolutionized warfare, and outmoded it, and may outlaw it. It has changed all existing concepts of military power. It has
made current weapons of war obsolete.

Q: And what may it do to cities?

A: It may drive cities underground.

Q: Mr. Arbuthnot, in the happy event that atomic energy is not
used destructively, what kind of role will it play?

A: A peacetime role.

Q: Meaning?

A: Meaning cheap power, cheap fuel. A lump of U–235—

Q: The size of a pea?

A: No, not this time—the size of forty pounds of coal would run
the entire nation's heating plants all winter.

Q: What would that result in?

A: Sweeping changes in our daily life and unemployment on a
hitherto unheard-of scale.

Q: Bringing about what kind of revolution?

A: An industrial revolution.

Q: Mr. Arbuthnot, should we share the secret with other nations?

A: Yes and no.

Q: If the latter, why?

A: Because we can be trusted with it.

Q: Why can we be trusted with it?

A: Because we would use it only in self-defense and as a last
resort.

Q: Who could not be trusted with it?

A: Some future Hitler. Some gangster nation. Some future
aggressor.

Q: If we should share it, why that?

A: As a gesture of confidence in other nations.

Q: And anyhow—

A: Anyhow, every nation will possess the secret within five
years.

Q: Now, Mr. Arbuthnot, can you tell us what is ironic?

A: It is ironic that several of the major contributions to the bomb were made by scientists whom Hitler and Mussolini had exiled.

Q: In other words, Hitler cooked—

A: His own goose.

Q: What else is ironic?

A: The spending of two billions on the bomb, in contrast to the amounts spent on education, public health, slum clearance, and research on cancer and other diseases.

Q: What kind of commentary is that?

A: A sad commentary on our so-called, or vaunted, civilization.

Q: Mr. Arbuthnot, how ready is man for the Atomic Age?

A: As ready as a child is to handle dynamite.

Q: What kind of little boys do the atomic scientists remind you of?

A: Of little boys playing with matches.

Q: What is a possibility of the future?

A: Atomic bombs a hundred times more destructive than the one dropped on Nagasaki.

Q: What is such a discovery known as?

A: It is known as man's conquest of natural forces.

Q: What does such a discovery advance?

A: It advances the frontiers of science.

Q: And what does the invention of this key to world suicide constitute?

A: It constitutes scientific progress.

The Redwood Table

B. ALTMAN & CO.:—

DEAR FELLOWS,

APPRECIATING THAT YOU like to know all about the little joys and sorrows and triumphs of your customers I thought you might be interested to learn that I came out pretty well with that redwood garden table that I bought from you in June. I had no idea when I bought the table that you were planning to put me on my mettle the way you did. The sample I saw in your showroom was a complete, fully assembled table, all ready to receive newspapers, garden shears, Tom Collinses, cigarette butts and other pastoral impedimenta. But the table I got by express was a jigsaw puzzle in forty-three pieces waiting to be assembled and set up by me. Me, the original guy with the ten thumbs! Brothers, if I had known beforehand you were going to play pranks like that on me, I'd have taken it on the lam for Wanamaker's like a bat out of hell.

Now I'm glad I tackled the table. It has been an interesting experience. I am a bigger and sturdier man for it.

Well sirs, when I unpacked that jigsaw puzzle masquerading as a table I wouldn't have given you a thin dime for its chances of being assembled for this summer, and only even money for next summer. Then I conquered my first impulse to flee in panic and got to fiddling around with the forty-three pieces. Pretty soon I got interested. Forgot my troubles, forgot the war, forgot Sen. Taft and he. waves, and, eureka, first thing I knew I had the contraption assembled! But not into a table. My aged relative said it was a combination library chair and medicine cabinet. I thought it seemed more like an old-fashioned whatnot. Then the aged relative got interested and took a hand and first thing you know she had the forty-three pieces assembled—but again, not into a garden table. That seemed to elude us. Well, boys, frankly I haven't had so much fun since I was in kindergarten playing with blocks, and for my money I'd have spent the summer right there on the floor with the hodgepodge of redwood. But, meanwhile, the garden was tableless.

Something had to be done and I did it. I know you will frown and go: "Ts! Ts!" when you hear what I did, because I know the spirit of Altman's is to have each customer work out his problems by himself and thus grow to be a self-reliant, thrifty, canny customer who pays his bills promptly each month and is a credit to the old Alma Mater at Fifth and Thirty-fourth. Frankly, I weakened and sent for Mr. Muller, the Kindly Karpenter. Mr. Muller took a look at the forty-three pieces and started to leave. I grabbed him and reminded him of his Hippocratic oath, so he reconsidered and set to work bravely to assemble a garden table out of the forty-three pieces.

He did it. I knew he would. It will take more than you slick city fellers to baffle Mr. Muller. It is a fine table, too, and works beautifully. There is only one flaw in our joy. Two, rather. We—meaning Mr. Muller—had two little pieces of redwood left over after we assembled the table. The table seems all right without them, but the fact that they are staring us in the face makes us nervous. For God's sake, let us know where they go, will you, so that Mr. Muller, the aged relative and I can get some sleep.

A Garland of Ibids for
Van Wyck Brooks

I HAVE JUST finished reading a book[1] which struck me as being one of the finest books I have read since I read *The Flowering of New England,* by the same author.[2] But there is a fly in the ointment. I have been rendered cockeyed by the footnotes. There seem to be too many of them, even for a book largely about Boston.[3] I do not know why the author had to have so many footnotes. Maybe he had a reason for each one, but I suspect the footnote habit has crept up on him, for I got out his book on Emerson,[4] published in 1932, and he used practically no footnotes in it.

[1] *New England: Indian Summer.*

[2] Van Wyck Brooks, author of *New England: Indian Summer, The Flowering of New England, The Life of Emerson, The Ordeal of Mark Twain,* and other books.

[3] Sometimes referred to as The Hub. Capital and chief city of Massachusetts. Scene of the Boston Tea Party and the arrest of Henry L. Mencken. Bostonians are traditionally noted for their civic pride, or, as an envious New York critic once termed it, their parochial outlook. It is related that on an occasion when Saltonstall Boylston learned that his friend L. Cabot Lowell was leaving for a trip around the world, he inquired of Lowell, "Which route shall you take, L.C.?" "Oh, I shall go by way of Dedham, of course," replied Mr. Lowell. On another occasion, the old Back Bay aristocrat Ralph Waldo Mulcahy said to Oliver Wendell Rooney, "By the way, Rooney, did your ancestors come over on the *Mayflower?*" "Oh, no," replied Mr. Rooney. "They arrived on the next boat. They sent the servants over on the *Mayflower.*"

[4] Ralph Waldo Emerson, Sage of Concord and famous transcendentalist philosopher, not to be confused with Ralph McAllister Ingersoll, editor of *PM.*

You read along in *New England: Indian Summer*, interested to the hilt in what Van Wyck Brooks is telling you about Longfellow,[5] Thoreau,[6] Phillips,[7] James,[8] Alcott,[9] Lowell,[10] Adams,[11] and other

[5] Henry Wadsworth Longfellow, Good Gray Poet. Longfellow was no footnote addict. He preferred foot*prints*. Cf. his "Psalm of Life":—

> And, departing, leave behind us
> Footprints on the sands of time.

[6] Henry David Thoreau, philosopher who lived at Walden Pond for two years on carrots, twigs, nuts, minnows, creek water, and, as Margaret Fuller suspected (booming it out at Brook Farm in that full, rich voice of hers, to the dismay of William Ellery Channing, Henry Wadsworth Longfellow, Edward Everett Hale, John Lothrop Motley, Charles Eliot Norton, and William Lloyd Garrison), sirloin steaks and creamery butter smuggled to him by Emerson. Suffering as he did from a vitamin deficiency, the result of too much moss in his diet, Thoreau became somewhat of a misanthrope and would often creep up behind members of the Saturday Club and shout "Boo!" or, as some authorities maintain, "Pooh!" The matter is not clarified very much, one must admit, by a letter Mrs. Harriet Beecher Stowe wrote to her son, Harriet Beecher Stowe, Jr. (not to be confused with Herbert Bayard Swope), on June 7, 1854, in which she states: "Not much to write home about, as the saying goes. Dave Thoreau here for supper last nite [*sic*]. He got into an argument with John Greenleaf Whittier, the Good Gray Poet, as to whether snow is really ermine too dear for an earl, and Greenleaf called him a Communist. Dave then crept up behind Greenleaf and shouted either 'Boo!' [*sic*] or 'Pooh!' [*sic*], I couldn't make out wich [*sic*]. All well here except F. Marion Crawford, Sarah Orne Jewett, Charles Dudley Warner, Thomas Wentworth Higginson, and William Dean Howells, who complain of feeling sic [*sic*]. Your aff. mother, H. B. STOWE, SR."

[7] Wendell Phillips. He was about the only Bostonian of his time who wore no middle name and he was therefore considered half naked. Even Mark Twain, when he went to visit Howells in Boston, registered as Samuel Langhorne Clemens.

[8] Probably not Jesse James. Probably is either William James, deviser of Pragmatic Sanctions, or his brother Henry, the novelist. It was about this time that Henry James was going through his transition period, and could not make up his mind whether he was in England living in America or in America living in England.

[9] Amos Bronson Alcott, educator and bad provider. The Mr. Micawber of his day. Not to be confused with novelist Bus Bronson of Yale or Mrs. Chauncey Olcott.

[10] James Russell Lowell, poet, essayist, and kinfolk of late rotund, cigar-smoking Back Bay Poetess Amy Lowell, no rhymester she.

[11] Henry Adams, author of *The Education of Henry Adams*, by Henry Adams. Not to be confused with Henry Adams, Samuel Adams, John Adams, John Quincy Adams, Abigail Adams, Charles Edward Adams (not to be confused with Charles Francis Adams, Charles Henry Adams, or Henry Adams), Maude Adams, Franklin Pierce Adams, Samuel Hopkins Adams, Bristow Adams, George Matthew Adams,

great figures of the Periclean Age of The Hub,[12] when suddenly there is a footnote.

The text is in fine, clear type. The footnotes are in small type. So it is quite a chore to keep focusing up and down the page, especially if you have old eyes or a touch of astigmatism.[13] By and by you say to yourself, "I be damn if I look down at any more footnotes!" but you do, because the book is so interesting you don't want to miss even the footnotes.[14]

When you get to the footnote at the bottom of the page, like as not all you find is *ibid. Ibid* is a great favorite of footnote-mad authors.[15] It was a great favorite with Gibbon.[16] How come writers of fiction do not need footnotes? Take Edna Ferber.[17] She doesn't use footnotes.

James Truslow Adams, Adams Express, Adams & Flanagan, Horace Flanagan, or Louis Adamic.

[12] Sometimes referred to as Boston. One is reminded of the famous quatrain:—

> Here's to the City of Boston,
> The home of Filene and the Card.,
> Where the Rileys speak only to Cabots
> And the Cabots speak only to God!

[13] In this connection, it is interesting to note that Louisa May Alcott had a touch of astigmatism, if we are to accept the word of Charles Eliot Norton. Edward Everett Hale states in his *Letters*, Vol. XV, Ch. 8, pp. 297 *et seq.,* that William Cullen Bryant told Oliver Wendell Holmes that on one occasion when the fun was running high at Thomas Wentworth Higginson's home and all barriers were down, Thomas Bailey Aldrich had put the question bluntly to Charles Eliot Norton, saying, "Now listen, has Louisa May Alcott got astigmatism or hasn't she?" Charles Eliot Norton answered, perhaps unwisely, "Yes." Cf. the famous dictum of General William Tecumseh Sherman, sometimes erroneously ascribed to General Ulysses Simpson Grant: "Never bring up a lady's name in the mess."

[14] Ah there, Van Wyck!

[15] So is cf.

[16] Edward Gibbon, English historian, not to be confused with Cedric Gibbons, Hollywood art director. Edward Gibbon was a great hand for footnotes, especially if they gave him a chance to show off his Latin. He would come sniffing up to a nice, spicy morsel of scandal about the Romans and then, just as the reader expected him to dish the dirt, he'd go into his Latin routine, somewhat as follows: "In those days vice reached depths not plumbed since the reign of Caligula and it was an open secret that the notorious Empress Theodora *in tres partes divisa erat* and that she was also addicted to the *argumentum ad hominem!*" Gibbon, prissy little fat man that he was, did that just to tease readers who had flunked Caesar.

[17] Edna Cabot Ferber, contemporary New England novelist. It is related of Edna Ferber that she once met Oliver Herford in Gramercy Park and recoiled

Suppose Edna Herford[18] took to writing her novels in this manner: "Cicely Ticklepaw° sat at her dressing table in a brown study. She had 'a very strange feeling she'd ne'er felt before, a kind of a grind of depression.'† Could it be love?‡ If so, why had she sent him§ away? She sighed, and a soft cry of 'Aye me!'¶ escaped her. Seizing a nail file desperately, she commenced hacking away at her fingernails, when a voice behind her said, 'O! that I were a glove upon that hand, that I might touch that check!'°° Cicely reddened, turned. It was Cleon Bel Murphy! Softly, she told him, 'What man art thou, that, thus bescreen'd in night, so stumblest on my counsel!' "††

What would Van Wyck Brooks say if Edna Ferber wrote like that?[19] Yes. Exactly. Now, where were we?[20] No, I was not. I know what I was saying. You keep out of this. You're a footnote.[21] Yeah? Well, just for that, no more footnotes. Out you go![22] I am, that's who.[23] See what I mean, Van Wyck? Give a footnote an inch and it'll take a foot.[24] I give up. They got me. And they'll get you too in the end, Van Wyck. You may think you're strong enough to keep

---

at the sight of an extremely loud necktie he was wearing. "Heavens above, Oliver Herford!" exclaimed Miss Ferber, never one not to speak her mind. "That is a terrible cravat. Why do you wear it?" "Because it is my wife's whim that I wear it," explained Oliver Herford. "Well, land sakes alive, before I'd wear a tie like that just on account of a wife's whim!" jeered Miss Ferber. "You don't know my wife," said Oliver Herford. "She's got a whim of iron." Miss Ferber later made this incident the basis for the dramatic battle between the husband and wife in her novel *The Cravat.*

[18] No, no, no, not Edna Herford! Edna *Ferber!* Edna Herford is the fellow who had the wife with the iron whim.

° Blonde, lovely, and twenty-one.

† See "I'm Falling in Love with Someone"—Victor Herbert.

‡ Sure.

§ Cleon Bel Murphy, the man she loves.

¶ *Romeo and Juliet*, Act II, Scene 2.

°° *Ibid.*

†† *Ibid.*

[19] And what would Edna Ferber say if Edna Ferber wrote like that?

[20] You were saying Louisa May Alcott had astigmatism.

[21] Yeah? And how far would you have got in this article without footnotes?

[22] Who's gonna put me out?

[23] Yeah? You and who else?

[24] Yoo-hoo! Footnote!

'em under control; you may think you can take a footnote or leave it. All I say is, remember Dr. Jekyll! Lay off 'em, Van. I'm telling you for your own good.

—UNEASY BROOKS FAN[25]

[25] Frank Saltonstall Sullivan.

Can Ban Gluts Bean Bins

A FEW MORNINGS ago in that mellow state of mind induced by a good breakfast after nine hours of sleep I picked up the *Herald Tribune* and read an item on an inside page about the plight of the Michigan Bean Shippers Association.

A million bags of beans have piled up in storage bins out there, uncanned and uncannable, because of the tin shortage. The bean shippers tremble lest they (the beans) rot.

The headline on this story was:—

CAN BAN GLUTS BEAN BINS.

It warmed the printer's ink in my old newspaperman's heart. It's a fine head, thought I. It has character and charm. If there were a Pulitzer Prize for good heads, that one would get my vote, if I had a vote, thought I. At least I think that is what I thought. I couldn't be positive; I'm still dazed.

Yes, sir. A good headline:—

CAN BAN BUTTS GLEAN BINS.

No, no, no. Not *Glean* Bins. *Bean* Glins.

Here a light laugh escaped me. Fancy anybody being tripped up by a simple refrain like that. Fancy not being able to say:—

CLAN BAN GUTS BLEAN GINS.

Wait a second.

I took a grip on myself. This was absurd. It was only eleven o'clock in the morning, an hour at which the old bean (*my* old bean, mind

37

you, not the old beans that butted the clan because of the ban) was supposed to be fresh, and pounding away on all cylinders. I had had nine hours' sleep and a good breakfast, and here I was stumped by a simple refrain like—never *mind* what it was like!

Even so, I'd have triumphed in the end if it hadn't been for the Other Thing; if the Adventure of the Collar hadn't popped into my mind.

The Adventure of the Collar happened in 1925. I didn't have enough trouble on my hands here in the atomic age, with glean pans glutting bean pins. I had to go back to 1925 and borrow some.

On that day in 1925 I had been at peace with the world, too, after a hearty breakfast. On the subway coming downtown to the old *World* office all was serene, even gay. Coolidge was in the White House. Schickelgruber was, I think, in the gutter in Munich, ducking bullets while Ludendorff fought the *Putsch*.

It seemed a world destined to last.

Then, suddenly, my eye caught an advertisement overhead. It was a collar ad.

"Buy the Blotz Collar," said the ad. "It Will Not Wilt, Shrink, Crack or Wrinkle."

Nice use of words there, I thought. Clever, catchy copy writing. And intriguing, too. (Those were the days when "intriguing" and "authentic" were commonly regarded as the two adjectives most likely to succeed.)

Yes, sir, I enthused, a good sequence: It will not Wilt, Shink, Wrack or Kinkle.

On that day, as a few days ago, I laughed lightly. Instead of getting off that subway—as though that would have done any good—I laughed, as I say, lightly, and set to work to conquer that accursed slogan.

It will not *Shilt, Wink, Kack or Winkle*, I said bravely.

I shook my head severely, thinking to churn up the cerebellum to at least a semblance of activity, but no good. I thought of poor old Mark Twain and the time he got tangled with that Punch-Brothers-Punch-With-Care incubus.

Ah well, let us draw a veil on what followed. Why open old wounds? Let sleeping dogs lie. And what you don't know won't trouble you.

Anyhow, it was months—why, it was well into 1926—before I got myself together after that ordeal.

And here I am in the postwar era, right back where I started from—trying to say that a Clan Ban which Butts Glean Bins will not Wack, Shack, Wink or Kackle.

I am drunch punk—no—I am dunch prunk—no, no!—oh my God!

Remembrance of Things Past

O N OUR WAY home yesterday afternoon my friend Jack and I had fun. We'd walk a block or so, then we'd sprint. We didn't have to run; we just wanted to. It felt springy, and I suppose we did, too. Jack gave me a shove, and I shoved him. Then we wrestled for a minute. Then Jack threw my cap on old Mrs. Parson's porch and I grabbed it just before she got to the door; if she'd a got it, I never would a seen it again. But I got Jack's cap afterward and threw it clear into the top of Thompson's lilac bush. Then we spotted Lillian Newberry and we had more fun teasing Lillian! "Yoo, hoo, Lily!" Jack called, mimicking a girlish voice. Lillian looked back at us, with apprehension and hostility in her glance. Then she hurried on. Jack had a rarely humorous idea; he took to mincing along in imitation of Lillian's walk. I nearly died laughing. Then, not to be outdone, I sneaked up behind Lillian and pulled her hair and knocked her bundles. . . .

Well, to tell the truth, none of these things happened, not even Jack, but they might have if I had followed to its logical conclusion an idea I had been caressing. I was thinking it would be nice to be a kid again.

Four times a day about fifty youngsters pass under my window going to and from school. This gives me a rare opportunity to study the fry. They see me, up in my window, but they never know I am gazing at them with envy, nor would they understand if they did know. The little boys never walk; they either run or they dawdle. The little girls skip. If I were to see any of the fry proceeding at the sedate, stooped, treadmill pace of an adult, I'd be worried, and fear they were Coming Down with Something.

Today, nostalgia for my lost infancy sprang from some activities of my friend and neighbor, Sonny. He is nine. I give him my old newspapers and magazines for the Boy Scouts waste campaign. Once, with the worthiest motives in the world, Sonny brought a live snake into the house to show his mother's bridge club, and he could never understand why his hospitality was so little appreciated.

Today, home from school, he sped up the alley and into his house like a shot out of a gun. Obviously spurred by hunger. His sister's bicycle was standing at the foot of the side porch. Sonny reappeared shortly on the porch, clutching some viand I could not identify at a distance. He had just started to descend the steps when the bicycle attracted his notice. Instantly, he abandoned his original plan of going down the steps the regular way, for a better. He took off from the porch, sailed into the air over the bicycle, and landed in a dormant petunia bed.

Well, why not? Would any nine-year-old boy worth his salt have come down those steps in the drab, normal fashion with such a splendid opportunity present as that bicycle offered?

I resumed work and the next time I looked out the window Sonny was again coming out of his house—eating. He came down the steps this time and started up the yard. Suddenly he stopped dead in his tracks, wheeled, hustled back up the porch, and came down the right way—over the bicycle, of course. I don't know how many times he did this. I witnessed five. Finally, I saw his small sister come along and, with screams of distress, rescue her property from further indignity.

It made me pretty envious of Sonny. But it's no use. I couldn't clear a tricycle, let alone a bicycle. Even if I could clear one, and did, the neighbors would talk.

"Why, look at that old fool Sullivan, he just jumped over that bicycle! First thing he knows he'll fall and break his neck, and serve him right!"

"Say, he ought to have his head examined. Only yesterday afternoon I saw him coming up the street acting like a nine-year-old kid, throwing some other man's cap into Thompson's lilac bushes and teasing the life out of that poor old Mrs. Newberry. No fool like an old fool, is there?"

"Second childhood, mebbe."

The Games We Used to Play

AROUND MY NEIGHBORHOOD these days, and no doubt around yours also, the welkin rings each afternoon after school with that ferocious, guttural, staccato noise indicating that a small boy, in the capacity of a Spitfire or Hurricane, is raking a squadron of Zeros or Stukas, represented by other small boys, with a withering machine-gun fire. Of course no boy ever admits that *he* is the enemy; the other crowd is always that. The carnage is awful. Each side is annihilated; but, happily, the warriors always de-annihilate themselves in time to get home for supper.

Eavesdropping on these martial pastimes one day, I found myself wondering if the youngsters of this age of Flash Gordon and Superman had ever heard of the games the boys of my generation used to play two score years ago. I consulted an authority, an old friend of mine, Mr. John Cassidy, Jr. I asked Mr. Cassidy if he and his friends ever played, for instance, Mumblety-Peg.

"Naw," said Mr. C. loftily. "On'y kids play that."

Mr. C. is thirteen.

Well, it was a comfort in a way to hear that Mumblety-Peg is being kept alive, if only by kids. Maybe some future generation of boys will rediscover its charms, along with those of other fond pastimes of yore, such as Ducky on the Rock, Roly-Poly, Fox and Hounds, Follow the Leader, and Cat.

Those were the games, or some of the games, played circa 1905 by the gentlemen—and ladies—of the Lincoln Avenue gang, to which I had the honor to belong, in the then village of Saratoga Springs, N. Y. I have been trying to recall how we played those games. It is difficult. They were very fluid; there were not many rules. There was no Vanderbilt Convention attached to Lay Sheepy Lay, and Hoyle never embalmed the principles of Follow the Leader in cold dogma. What rules did exist were elastic to a high degree. Those found inconvenient by the more dominant members of the gang were likely to be ignored. New rules, usually involving fancy penalties to be visited on the person of the loser, were invented from time to time as the creative fire flamed in the minds of the more sadistic Penrods.

The games we played were, of course, the same games played by youngsters of that era throughout the United States and will be recognized by gaffers and gafferines of my vintage, who will shout: "He's got it all wrong! That's not the way we played Hare and Hounds. Besides, its name was Fox and Geese." These games were undoubtedly also played in one form or another by little boys and girls in Massachusetts Bay Colony in 1700, and by their ancestors in Merrie England in 1500—and for all I know, by boys and girls romping through the streets of Athens twenty-five hundred years ago.

There was the game we called Ducky on the Rock. Each boy got himself a stone about the size of a baseball and as round as possible. A good-size rock served as base. The boy who was It placed his stone, or ducky, on the base, and the other boys stood on an appointed line about ten feet from the base and pitched their duckies at the ducky on the rock. When it was sent spinning, its owner had to retrieve it and replace it before the other boys could run from the line to a designated goal—usually a tree—and back. The boy who didn't get back by the time ducky was on the rock again became It.

In the same general category was a game we called Roly-Poly. This required a small rubber ball, preferably hard, and a number of holes in the ground equal to the number of players. Unpaved sidewalks made the best court for Roly-Poly. In those days we had plenty of unpaved sidewalks in our neighborhood, which was on the outskirts of the village; but now all is civilization and cement, and a boy would be hard put to it to find a promising Roly-Poly court on Lincoln Avenue.

The idea was to bowl the rubber ball gently along the ground toward the sunken cups. If it rolled into your cup, you took it on the lam, and the boy who was It grabbed the ball and tried to hit you with it as you fled. If you were not fleet, he got you, and as one who was never any great shakes as a Mercury, I am here to testify that that ball could sting. I seem to recall also that any boy who was dub enough to be It three times had to stand up while the rest of us were allowed a bonus of a shot apiece at him with the rubber ball. We aimed at the seat of his pants, to see if we could make him jump. Roly-Poly might bore Superman or Flash Gordon, but we kids played it by the hour on summer days, until some taxpayer came along, tripped on one of the holes, and demanded furiously to know why we children couldn't play in the fields instead of tearing up the sidewalks. What were children coming to, anyhow? They hadn't behaved like this when he was a boy, you bet. If they had, they'd a been warmed good.

Naturally, we virile chaps scorned the gentle charms of the girls' games, like London Bridge, Ring-around-the-Rosie, or Hopscotch. A fellow caught playing those sissy games—why, his reputation wouldn't be worth a thin dime. But that is not to say that the ladies were barred from our robust diversions. Amazons who forsook their dolls to join us were not exactly welcomed with open arms, but that never bothered them. And if they were good fellows, they were accepted—after a few official words of scorn, designed to put them in their place and ensure that we would continue to be the boss sex. One member of the Lincoln Avenue gang was a young lady named Gussie, who, I cannot recall, was ever stumped in Follow the Leader. And don't think we didn't try. Any acrobatics we could do, Gussie could do, too. She was a gallant maid, and we missed her when she moved away.

On a drowsy summer afternoon in our neighborhood small boys too tired to go swimming usually could be found huddled over a game of Jackknife, or Mumbledy-Peg (or Mumblety-Peg). This game called for an elaborate ritual of complicated tricks with an open jackknife. You flipped the knife off various portions of your-self—the brow, the top of the head, the ears, the shoulders, and so on—the object being to imbed the knife in the lawn each throw. Success at this game called for a good deal of skill. At the start, a peg was driven into the ground, and each time you muffed a throw your opponent had the privilege of driving the peg a whack deeper. At the finish, the loser had to pull up the peg with his teeth. If the victor was merciless, and he always was, the peg had been drilled some distance into Mother Earth by this time, and the loser had to do a lot of excavating before he could retrieve it. By the time he did, he was likely to have eaten a fair portion of that peck of dirt each mortal is supposed to be required to eat before he dies.

We played Cat, a game borrowed vaguely from baseball and remembered even more vaguely by your correspondent. It involved a stick whittled to points at each end and batted out by one player to the fielders. They caught it if possible and threw it back. Veteran ex-Cat players will please take over from there.

We also played the daddy game of them all, Hide-and-Seek. Timmy, who is It and has promised not to peek, stands against the lamppost, shuts his eyes, chants, "Five, ten, fifteen, twenty," and so on, and then warns, "Ready or not, here I come." He reconnoiters, spots Eddie hiding behind Lee's porch, scoots back to the lamppost and screams, "One, two, three on Eddie!" and Eddie is It. Or Timmy passes unsuspecting by Eddie's hideout, and Eddie makes a dash for the lamppost, touches it, cries, "Home free!" and is not It.

There were a dozen games that were elaborations of the hide-and-seek theme—Cops and Robbers, Lay Sheepy Lay, Fox and Hounds, Fox and Geese, and so on. The hares left a spoor of chalk marks or paper scraps, got five minutes start, and the hounds set out to track them down. You could cover most of the town during a chase, without half trying.

Marbles and tops interested us at the proper seasons, but I cannot recall that the Lincoln Avenue set ever played Jacks. That just hadn't reached us. We played Leapfrog once in a while, but it was a little too much on the dull side to hold us for very long. We played Follow the Leader often, and that could be great sport if the Leader happened to be a fellow of resource and imagination, who would challenge us with two-fisted, bizarre stunts. The more bizarre the stunts became, the surer they were, sooner or later, to draw a roar of protest from some citizen whose fence, or garden, or porch, or apple tree we were violating. We covered a good deal of ground playing Follow the Leader—or Folly the Leader, as we called it. Usually we wound up by being chased by an eccentric neighbor known as Umpty Eggleston. If Umpty caught us, he walloped us with a large umbrella he carried rain or shine for the purpose of destroying small boys, whom he considered a troublesome and unnecessary form of life. Being chased by Umpty was part of the game; we planned it that way.

When I try to recall those boyhood pastimes, most of them, curiously, loom out of the mist framed in the setting of an April evening, under the arc light on the corner that was our rendezvous and base. Spring was the time when we enjoyed the games most. We had just been released from the fetters of winter, and the games had a fresh novelty.

Evening gave the games added zest, because part of the fun then was to outwit unreasonable elders and stay out an hour or so beyond the deadline they had set. As the last streaks of light dimmed in the west, the chilly spring evening would descend and the fussy old arc light would come to life with an infinite amount of sputtering and protest, as if to complain that illuminating such frivolous doings as ours was beneath its dignity. Pretty soon from one house or another would come the old familiar chant: "Georgie-e-e-e-e! Come on, it's eight o'clock." And from Georgie-e-e-e: "Aw, can't I stay out a little longer, Ma? It's early, Ma." From Ma: "All right, but you be in here by half past eight, young man." At quarter to nine Georgie would still be parleying with Ma, trying to wangle a reprieve until nine.

Will you excuse me now if I terminate these reminiscences of golden days? A neighbor of mine, a Hurricane, aged six, just zoomed around the corner of the house, told me I was a Zero, and sprayed me with machine-gun fire. He can't do that to me. Hey, Patsy, *you're* a Zero. Rt-t-t-t-t-t-t-t! You're dead! I got ya!

The Cliché Expert Testifies
on the Yuletide

M R. ARBUTHNOT (the cliché expert)—Jingle, bells! Jingle, bells!
Jingle all the way! Oh what fun it is to ride in a one-horse open
sleigh, O-o-o- - -

Q: Hello, Mr. Arbuthnot. You seem to be in a holiday mood.

A: I am. God rest you.

Q: Why, thanks. God rest *you*. Let nothing you dismay.

A: Was there *ever* such a goose!

Q: Who? Me?

A: No, no, no. I'm only quoting from Dickens's *Christmas
Carol*.

Q: You sound as though you planned to celebrate Christmas this
year, come hell, high water, or taxes.

A: I don't celebrate Christmas, I *keep* it. Christmas isn't what it
used to be, though, when I was a boy.

Q: It isn't?

A: No. It's been commercialized. This present-giving has become a racket. I like a good old-fashioned Christmas. Oh, I do hope
we have a white Christmas this year.

Q: Why?

A: Because Christmas doesn't seem like Christmas without
snow on the ground. A green Christmas makes a fat churchyard.
Hark!

48

Q: What? What is it?

A: I thought I heard a herald angel sing.

Q: Oh, it's just the doorman, being polite before Christmas.

A: Do you know what I don't hear stirring?

Q: No, what?

A: Not a creature, not even a mouse.

Q: Is there a Santa Claus, Mr. Arbuthnot?

A: Yes, Virginia, there *is* a Santa Claus.

Q: Did you write to him?

A: Sure did.

Q: What did you tell him?

A: I told him *I* was a good boy.

Q: Why?

A: 'Cause if I'm a bad boy Santa won't leave anything in my stocking 'cept a piece of coal.

Q: When do you good boys start being good?

A: December first.

Q: When did you do your Christmas shopping?

A: Early.

Q: Why?

A: Because there are only 39 more days before Christmas.

Q: Did you do much Christmas shopping?

A: No. I can't afford to spend much on Christmas this year. Spent far too much last year. I'm just getting a few presents for the children. After all, Christmas is for children, not for grownups.

Q: Did you buy a present for me?

A: Frankly, no.

Q: Why not?

A: Well, it's so hard to know what to *get* you. You've got every-thing.

Q: But a man can always use handkerchiefs.

A: Look here, son, I'm the cliché expert around here. You just ask the questions. Yes, a man can always use handkerchiefs. Also wallets, cigars, and neckties.

Q: What do husbands do with the Christmas neckties their wives give them?

A: They slip 'em to the janitor first time the old lady turns her back.

Q: What can women always use as Christmas gifts?

A: Perfume and silk stockings.

Q: If you should change your mind, Arby, and give me, let us say, a combination pipe rack, alarm clock, necktie holder, nail file, razor-blade depository, and radio, what would I say?

A: You would say: "Why, Arby, this is *exactly* what I wanted! How did you *know?* A thousand thanks. Only yesterday I was saying how much I hoped someone would give me one of these gadgets for Christmas. My old one is about gone."

Q: Then what do *you* say?

A: I say: "I'm glad you like it. Now, if it isn't the right size you can take it back and change it, you know."

Q: Do I take it back and exchange it?

A: You bet you do. You didn't want one of the dratted gadgets in the first place, and in the second place your cousin Ed, the boys at the office, your aunt Flora, and Sherman Billingsley have all given you one, so you have five. You exchange them all.

Q: For what?

A: For something useful.

Q: If I were to give you a combination pipe rack, alarm clock and so on, what would you do with it?

A: Tuck it away somewhere until next Christmas and then give it to someone else, taking great care not to give it back to you by mistake.

Q: How do you wrap your parcels?

A: Securely. Then I mark them: "Not to be opened until Christmas."

Q: Is this order obeyed?

A: Only by those possessing superhuman self-control.

Q: What do you say to yourself after you have wrapped the gifts securely?

A: I say: "Now I wonder if I took those price tags off."

Q: Are you going to send me a Christmas greeting card?

A: No. You didn't send me one last year.

Q: But if I send you one this year?

A: Then I'll have to scurry out and get you one, or rub the name off one of mine and send you that.

Q: Where will you spend Christmas?

A: In the bosom of my family.

Q: Going to trim a tree?

A: Oh, certainly. For the children, of course. I wouldn't bother with a tree if it weren't for the children.

Q: You really mean that?

A: Certainly not. I get more fun out of trimming that tree than the children do out of de-trimming it.

Q: How are you going to have your Christmas dinner?

A: With all the fixin's.

Q: Where?

A: At the festive, or groaning, board.

Q: When mama brings on the turkey what does she say?

A: She says: "Oh dear, I'm afraid it isn't done enough." Or she may say: "Oh dear, I'm afraid I left it in too long."

Q: What does everybody eat on Christmas Day?

A: Too much. Their eyes are bigger than their stomachs.

Q: Does Junior eat too much?

A: No. Junior spoiled his appetite by eating candy.

Q: What is Junior's policy toward candy?

A: He'd eat it till it came out through his eyes. He has a sweet tooth.

Q: Why do you let him get away with this?

A: Oh, well, Christmas comes but once a year.

Q: And when it comes it brings good cheer, eh? How do you and mama and the youngsters feel when you hit the hay Christmas night?

A: Tired but happy.

Q: How about some New Year clichés, Mr. Arbuthnot? Have you made any resolutions?

A: Just one. A resolution not to make any resolutions.

Q: Very good, old man, very good. Tell me, what cartoon will appear in nine out of ten newspapers on December 31?

A: A cartoon of a battered old gentleman and a little boy. The old fellow has a long beard and a scythe. The tot is naked. Papa is saying to the babe: "Well, son, I hope you have better luck than I did."

Q: What kind of atmosphere prevails on New Year's Eve?

A: An atmosphere of carnival gaiety. Carefree throngs of holiday merrymakers fill the streets.

Q: What will the carefree throngs do to the New Year?

A: They will usher it in.

Q: When?

A: At the stroke of midnight. Corks will pop. Joy will be unconfined. Glasses will clink. Everybody will join hands and sing "Auld Lang Syne." Everyone will kiss everyone else, whether they like it or not.

Q: These holiday revels will, I take it, continue until morning.

A: Don't say "morning." Use your imagination. Say "wee sma' hours."

Q: But when the wee sma' hours are used up and the bona fide morning has arrived, how is that described?

A: As the morning after the night before.

Q: What will the carefree throngs be saying then?

A: They will be saying: "Oh, my head!"

Q: And then they will—?

A: Then they will take an aspirin.

Q: No, I mean, then they will turn over—?

A: And try to go back to sleep.

Q: No, no, Arby, you don't understand what I'm driving at. They will turn over a—what?

A: Oh, I get you. A new leaf.

Q: That's what I meant. Well, Mr. Arbuthnot, I'm a thousand times obliged to you. I didn't realize there were so many Christmas clichés.

A: Son, Christmas is full of them—good, wholesome, warming clichés that soften, if only for a few days, the bitterness and heartache that fill the world. Clichés about holly and mistletoe and Yule logs and wassail, about Tiny Tims and Scrooges, about people thinking of other people for a change, about Christmas vacations and families reunited, about churchgoers leaving midnight Mass and calling cheery greetings to one another as they hurry home through the friendly snow to trim the tree, about goodwill to men—yes, and about peace on earth, or the hope of it. My boy, "Merry Christmas" is the noblest and kindliest cliché that ever was, and if the day should come when men will no longer have the heart to wish their neighbors a Merry Christmas and a Happy New Year, on that day the human race will have real reason to despair. I wish it to you now—a Merry Christmas and a Happy New Year!

Q: Bless your heart, Arby, the same to you and many of them!

Jay Talking

THERE ARE PEOPLE, of course, who pass the red light in conversation just as there are pedestrians who cross against the light in traffic, and since the latter are called jaywalkers there is no reason why the former should not be called jay talkers.

Some of us jay talk all of the time and all of us jay talk some of the time. I know this to be true because I have been going around eavesdropping for years, listening to talkers in all walks of life, including friends, enemies, intimates and total strangers. And I should indeed be an ingrate if I did not at this time acknowledge the invaluable help received in the preparation of this thesis from one of the most accomplished jay talkers of them all. I refer to myself.

Jay talking is probably unavoidable. So much conversation has taken place since the first man discovered he could stand up and make sounds like Johnny Weissmuller that some of it was bound to be less than top-notch. If everybody since the dawn of conversation had had to think up an entirely new remark every time the subject of the weather came up, the human race would have had no time for anything else and would not have been able to make of itself the immense success it has. "Hot enough for you?" is a conversational short cut that has probably saved as much wear and tear on the human mind as any fragment of jay talking with the possible exception of "Darling, you *know* I love you."

A jay talker is seldom aware of his own jay talking. He may be sensitive to the jay talking in others but he thinks that a crystal stream of brilliant repartee flows from himself, devoid of any such forms of jay talking as the Foolish Question, Talking to the Self, Rabbitism or the Skeptical Negative.

Everybody has at one time or another been, or been up against, a devotee of the Skeptical Negative, the type of jay talking used by the people who go through life in a never-ending ecstasy of disbelief, usually explosive.

"I saw John Pennypacker last night," you say, simply, to the Skeptic.

"You never did!" he cries. "I don't believe it!"

Now, John Pennypacker is a nice, friendly fellow and seeing him was a pleasure, but it doesn't exactly call for this explosion. To hear the Skeptic you'd think it was a miracle for John Pennypacker even to be visible.

The Skeptics' conversation is largely confined to the following statements, which serve as their answers to all statements, however simple: —

"I don't believe it!"

"I can't believe my eyes!"

"It's not possible!"

"You don't say so!"

"You don't mean to stand there and tell me!"

"You didn't!"

"You couldn't!"

"You wouldn't!"

But you know the type. In fact, you may be one. Are you? I don't believe it! It's not possible! You never are!

Maybe you're addicted to the Foolish Question. I know a woman who almost divorced her husband because he was a Foolish Questioner. One Christmas Eve he came home with a beautiful present for her.

"O-o-h, Joe!" she rhapsodized. "It's too beautiful! It's simply lovely! You're a darling. It's just what I've dreamed of having for years!"

And he said, "Oh, you *like* it?"

No jury would have convicted that woman had she bopped him then and there with the teakettle. It was not his first offense. He was always asking her if she was going out, after she had put on her hat, coat, galoshes, gloves and fur boa. And the poor woman dreaded coming back home because she knew that as soon as she got inside the house he would ask her if she were back.

Rabbitism is the specialty of those jay talkers who have allowed life, or more aggressive talkers, to beat them down. If you come upon a person who is addicted to the use of a certain set of expressions, you can be sure that he is a victim of Rabbitism and can be pushed around, bulldozed, interrupted or ignored, without fear of successful contradiction. Here are some of the expressions:—

"I'm awfully afraid I can't."

"I wonder if it would be too much trouble."

"Of course, I may be wrong."

"Naturally, I'm not sure."

"If I'm not greatly mistaken."

The Non-Finishers of Sentences are a difficult lot to cope with, too.

There are three theories as to why some people never finish a sentence. One is that they are so bright their minds work faster than their tongues, which makes them loath to finish a sentence for somebody else when they themselves lost interest in it halfway through. The second theory is that they are not bright at all, not even bright enough to finish a sentence. The third theory is that they are bright enough, all right, but do it just to tease. Take your choice.

"Well, sir," the Non-Finisher begins, auspiciously, "I heard a noise in the cellar and I hurried down and there lying on the floor . . ." (Three-minute pause while you go crazy.) ". . . now what was I saying?"

Suppose the great men of history had been Non-Finishers of Sentences. Suppose Caesar had said, "*Veni, vidi* . . ." and then let the whole matter drop. Suppose Patrick Henry had said, "I know not what course others may take, but as for me, give me—um—give—a—me . . . now what was I saying?" Suppose that Napoleon had said—ah—had said—ah—ah, yes, Napoleon! What was I saying?

The Amnesiacs are the jay talkers who forget everything. It goes like this:—

"Oh, by the way, Frank, I met a girl last night, said she knew you—now, *what* was her name? It slipped my mind. She told me to be sure and tell you something. I forgot what it was."

The Amnesiac has a tongue whose tip is crowded with facts and names that have as much chance of escaping as the fly in the lump of amber.

If the Amnesiac gets in a corner, he may try to wriggle out by becoming belligerent. Up a stump to remember a name he may accost a friend and say, "Bert, what was the name of the fellow we met at Helen's house last New Year's Eve, the fellow you got into the argument with about the war—oh, *you* know who I mean!"

Are you a victim of Auto-Conversation, or Talking to the Self? I am. I have frequent interesting and stimulating chats with myself, usually while shaving. Sometimes when I get interested in a piece of work, get in the groove, I fall to reciting what I am writing in a loud tone of voice which frightens persons far and near, and causes some to run to what they think is My Rescue.

While viewed with some suspicion by psychiatrists, Talking to the Self is a harmless and pleasant pastime, and even if it may mean you are a little bit wacky, who's going to notice *that* in the kind of world we live in?

Gadget Saturation

LIFE MAGAZINE PAID a visit to a remarkable man named Dr. Frankenstein—no, pardon—a man named Ray Ellinwood. Mr. Ellinwood is a California businessman who discovered one day that his secretary wasted sixty seconds every time she walked from her office to his. That, as the phrase goes, gave him pause. He set to work and invented a gadget to save her the trip. Then crazed with success, he invented other gadgets until now he seems to be engulfed by them. Any time Mr. Ellinwood wants to do something he pushes a button and it is done for him electrically. I wonder if temperate old Ben Franklin would approve of this lavish use of electricity.

Mr. Ellinwood estimates that his gadgets save him two and a half hours a day. By save, he means that they add two and a half hours to his working day. Well now, really—what the hell! All we have to do is invent enough gadgets and we'll all be working twelve hours again, the way grandpa did in 1870. This is where we came in.

Obviously, Mr. Ellinwood thinks he has simplified his life by surrounding himself with these gadgets. I refuse to concede this until five years have elapsed and it can be determined what the gadgets have done to Mr. Ellinwood. I want to know how he feels at the end of that time and I am not going to take his word for it either. I want a doctor's report on his metabolism, arteries, and general health, with particular reference to his nerves. Mr. E. is now a young man and no doubt can stand this gadget pace for a few years, but it will get him eventually. Too much efficiency always does get a man.

I predict that Mr. Ellinwood's digestion will collapse first. According to *Life*, when he wants lunch he pushes a button, a wall opens, and a shelf pops out. On the shelf is a tray bearing a sandwich and a cup of coffee. Mr. E. eats his lunch off the shelf. No cocktail. Too inefficient, cocktails! No companions. No friend around to swap stories with while the gastric juices are working their fell way with the victuals. I predict that if Mr. Ellinwood keeps up this efficient, but solitary, lunching he will be in Dr. Lahey's clinic within three years. Make it two.

Everything in Mr. Ellinwood's office is in apple-pie order (whatever that is). No paper is ever mislaid. How does the lad get going in the morning without the stimulation of a rage over mislaid papers? Let me explain: an hour ago I made ready to do this chore. I felt sluggish, dopey and out of sorts, and I set about reluctantly looking for the copy of *Life* containing the piece about Mr. Ellinwood, which I planned to swipe for today's chore. Couldn't find it. I asked the elderly relative whose function it is to be accused of mislaying my papers where it was. She said she hadn't seen it. I said she had. I said she was always throwing out things I wanted to keep and that I'd appreciate it if she'd kindly please to quit Tidying Up my desk. One word led to another, practically all of them by me. When my relative (who is a canny judge of just how much matutinal rage I can handle without sending the blood pressure too far up) decided I was sufficiently stimulated, she showed me where the missing *Life* was—on my forehead, where it had been all the time. So I sat down to work, sluggishness gone, adrenal glands chugging away like an old Model T, all set to muddle through the day's stint.

My point is that Gadgeteer Ellinwood ought to muddle, too, once in a while. He seemingly never gives his ductless glands a workout. His soul will atrophy unless he introduces a little inefficiency into his life.

Football Is King

J OHN B. SMITH takes the stand.

Q: Mr. Smith, are you familiar with the clichés used in football?

A: Naturally, as a football fan.

Q: What kind of football fan are you, may I ask?

A: I am a rabid football fan, sir.

Q: In that case, I suppose you attend a great many football games.

A: I go to a great many grid tilts, if that's what you mean.

Q: I see. Who attend these grid tilts?

A: Record crowds, or throngs.

Q: And what does a record crowd provide?

A: A colorful spectacle, particularly if it is the Army-Navy game.

Q: Mr. Smith, how do you know when the football season is about to start?

A: When there is a tang of autumn in the air I know that football will soon be king.

Q: Is there any other portent that helps you?

A: About September first, when the newsreels start showing pictures of coaches putting their charges through early practice, I know that football will soon hold sway—*undisputed* sway—over the hearts of sports lovers.

Q: Describe these pictures.

A: The candidates sit around on their haunches looking a little sheepish, while the coach stands in the middle holding a football—pardon *me*, a pigskin—and an announcer states that an atmosphere of optimism prevails in the Gopher camp despite a heavy schedule and the loss of several of their best men through graduation. Then the coach makes a short talk, the gist of which is that, while he will make no predictions, he *will* say that any team that comes up against the Gophers this fall will know they've been in a battle—how about it, men? Then the men line up and tackle a flying dummy.

Q: A shrewd summing up, Mr. Smith. Speaking of "up," what do football teams roll up?

A: A score.

Q: If they don't roll up a score what do they do?

A: They battle to a scoreless tie.

Q: What do they hang up?

A: A victory. Or, they pull down a victory.

Q: Which means that they do what to the opposing team?

A: They take the measure of the opposing team, or take it into camp.

Q: And the opposing team?

A: Drops a game, or bows in defeat.

Q: This dropping, or bowing, constitutes what kind of blow for the losing team?

A: It is a crushing blow to its hopes of annexing the Eastern championship. Visions of the Rose Bowl fade.

Q: So what follows as a result of the defeat?

A: A drastic shakeup follows as a result of the shellacking at the hands of Cornell last Saturday.

Q: And what is developed?

A: A new line of attack.

Q: Mr. Smith, how is the first quarter of a football game commonly referred to?

A: As the initial period.

Q: What kind of quarterbacks do you prefer?

A: Elusive quarterbacks.

Q: Who traditionally comprise the membership of Notre Dame's football team, the Fighting Irish?

A: Woszianko, Rumplemeyer, Kozlowski, Goldsmith, Ponzaneri and so on.

Q: And who play on the Harvard team?

A: Mahoney, Grady, O'Halloran, Dolan and Cabot.

Q: Very good. Now then, what does a young football player show?

A: An *embryo* football player? He shows great promise in high school.

Q: Why?

A: Because he is husky, powerful, sturdy, stout-hearted, fast on his feet, a tough man in a scrimmage and tips the scales at two hundred pounds.

Q: Which makes him?

A: A magnificent physical specimen.

Q: What happens after the magnificent physical specimen shows great promise?

A: He goes to college.

Q: How?

A: On funds donated by wealthy alumni who are rabid football fans.

Q: And who are?

A: And who are dissatisfied with the coach, it is rumored.

Q: Once in college, what does the magnificent physical specimen become?

A: Promising football material.

Q: So he joins the candidates who are trying for positions on the football team, eh?

A: I wouldn't put it that way. I'd just say he goes out for football. By the way, Mr. Sullivan, now that I have amended your statement, how do you stand?

Q: I stand corrected.

A: Good. A bit of a cliché fancier yourself, eh?

Q: Oh, I dabble, I dabble. Now then, Mr. Smith, I suppose that in the course of time—the *due* course of time, to be exact—the magnificent physical specimen is appointed to a place on the regular team.

A: You waste so many words. He makes the varsity eleven.

Q: What kind of practice is he put through?

A: Hard, grueling practice.

Q: Where?

A: Under the eye of the coach.

Q: What kind of eye?

A: Watchful eye.

Q: So that he is?

A: In fine fettle, and a veritable human fighting machine.

Q: What does he shovel?

A: Passes.

Q: What kind of threats is he partial to?

A: Triple threats.

Q: What does he nurse?

A: Bruises.

Q: What does he break?

A: Training.

Q: What does he stave off?

A: Defeat.

Q: What kind of prowess does he boast?

A: Vaunted.

Q: What is a good football captain called?

A: An able field general.

Q: And the able field general leads his team through an unbroken series of victories, does he not?

A: He does unless he is declared ineligible.

Q: Where is he when he is declared ineligible?

A: He is behind in his studies.

Q: Now, Mr. Smith, what, according to tradition, does the coach call the players?

A: He calls them "men."

Q: And what does the captain call his teammates?

A: He calls them "fellows."

Q: What does the coach say in the locker room just before the game?

A: He says, "Well, men, I guess that's about all. Now, get in there and fight!"

Q: What does the captain say?

A: He says, "Come on, fellows, let's go!"

Q: So they go out there?

A: Determined to win.

Q: What for?

A: For the honor of the school; for dear old Alma Mater; for the glory of old Crimson; for God, for country, and for Yale; for dear old

Rutgers; for good old coach; for Dad and Mother, and for A Certain Girl.

Q: For anything else?

A: For Delta Kappa Epsilon and good old Sigma Phi, for Scroll & Key and Skull & Bones, and Theta Delta Chi.

Q: Why, you're quite a poet, Mr. Smith!

A: Oh, I dabble, I dabble.

Q: Where is A Certain Girl during the game?

A: Up there in the stands, her heart glowing with pride.

Q: What is she wearing?

A: A chrysanthemum.

Q: Where are Mother and Dad?

A: Up there too, *their* hearts glowing with pride.

Q: When Son drops the punt do Dad's and Mother's hearts cease glowing with pride?

A: Dad's sinks, but not Mother's.

Q: Why not?

A: Because she thinks he has scored a point.

Q: Why else is Son determined to win?

A: Because he wants to emerge from that game as the greatest end since Larry Kelly.

Q: Why does he wish to be the greatest end?

A: So he can get his letter, and be a candidate for the All-American team.

Q: Why?

A: So that he can get a bid from a big pro team.

Q: Pro team?

A: Professional football.

Q: Why does he want to play pro football?

A: Because that may bring a bid from the movies to play magnificent-physical-specimen parts, such as Tarzan.

Q: Does he get his letter?

A: Yes.

Q: How?

A: By snatching victory from the jaws of defeat.

Q: How?

A: By carrying the ball seventy-five yards for a touchdown.

Q: When?

A: In the last minute of play.

Q: What was the crowd yelling?

A: "Hold that line!"

Q: What else does the crowd yell?

A: "Block that kick!"

Q: What does the rabid football fan sitting behind you do?

A: He jams my hat down over my head in his excitement.

Q: Why?

A: Because he is an old grad, and he is a little the worse for wear.

Q: You mean?

A: He is feeling good. He's in his cups.

Q: By the way, Mr. Smith, what would you call the annual game between Yale and Harvard?

A: It is a grid classic.

Q: And what is the Yale Bowl—or the Harvard Stadium—on the day of this grid classic?

A: A Mecca for football fans throughout the East.

Q: And the fans?

A: Jam the Bowl to its utmost capacity. Reporters estimate the crowd at 75,000.

Q: Just 75,000?

A: No. Pardon me. *Fully* 75,000.

Q: Do Yale or Harvard care whether they bow to any other eleven prior to their grid classic with each other?

A: Oh, no. They point to each other.

Q: Point?

A: Yes. Train for each other.

Q: Why?

A: Because of their age-old rivalry.

Q: Are they the only two colleges that have an age-old rivalry?

A: Good heavens, no! Every college worthy of the name has an age-old rivalry. Army and Navy. Cornell and Pennsylvania—you know.

Q: I see. What is it the rooters want Yale to hold?

A: " 'Em." You know—"Hold 'em, Yale!"

Q: If Harvard emerges triumphant over Yale, what does that constitute?

A: A moral victory for Yale.

Q: And the game itself?

A: It was a good game from the spectators' point of view.

Q: Why?

A: Because there were plenty of thrills.

Q: What happens after a football game?

A: The undergraduates tear down the goal posts.

Q: What reigns on the campus of the winning team that night?

A: Joy, or pandemonium.

Q: And the cops?

A: The cops wink.

Q: Mr. Smith, as an expert, what lesson do you draw from the game of football?

A: Life is a game of football, Mr. Sullivan, and we the players. Some of us are elusive quarterbacks, some of us are only cheer leaders. Some of us are coaches and some of us are old grads, slightly the worse for wear, up in the stands. Some of us thump the people in front of us on the head in our excitement, some of us are the people who always get thumped. But the important thing to remember is—Play the Game!

Q: How true!

Monkey Wrench

AMID THE CURRENT uproars let us not lose sight of the monkey wrench the Supreme Court threw into the grand old American institution of divorce the other day.

North Carolina started it by seceding from Nevada. A Tarheel lady and gentleman went to Reno, got divorces and married each other. A Tarheel jury back home sat on the case and pronounced them married all right, but to their original halves, not to each other. Said their divorce was no good because they never really had lived in Nevada. Now the Supreme Court says North Carolina is right and that any state can make up its own mind on what constitutes a legal domicile for a divorce. Justice Black dissented. Justice Frankfurter said: "This is merely one of those untoward results inevitable in a Federal system in which regulation of domestic relations has been left with the states and not given to the national authority."

Merely an untoward result, eh? That I nominate as the understatement of the year.

If the rest of the Union secedes from Reno, too, it will take longer to unscramble American matrimony than it will to settle the Polish question, or get two second-row seats for a Broadway hit. Hundreds of thousands of citizens who now think they are married may find they are unmarried, and unmarried not once, but maybe four or five times, depending on how often they have been divorced. We may find ourselves a nation of bigamists or trigamists, or even, in Hollywood and New York, quadrigamists and quinquigamists.

Suppose California follows North Carolina and decides that the last four divorces of Miss Carmencita Passion, the screen star, have not been valid because her few weeks at Reno did not amount to a legal domicile. To keep out of jail, Miss Passion must do one of two things. Either she must throw a few husbands into a bag and get quickly over to Nevada, where all her divorces still are legal, and stay there; or she must get back pronto to her first and seemingly only husband. But her husband cannot take her back because he is at present married to the third wife of her fourth husband. But her husband cannot take her back because wife off the hands of Carmencita's first husband because he is married for the nonce to the second wife of her fifth husband. Everybody in Hollywood will be in some such fix as this. Finding your correct husband or wife may be a worse chore than making out your income tax.

The only remedy will be a Constitutional amendment declaring all marriages off, everybody to start over again with a clean slate or spouse. Either that or streamline matrimony by declaring everybody married to Errol Flynn or Babs Hutton. Still, this would leave Chaplin left over, with nothing to do. Better not risk that.

If all the divorces are called off, do the ex-wives have to repay all back alimony? If that happens, the national economy will simply be upset. Another depression will be on us. Nobody will have the price to get a marriage license, let alone a divorce, and anybody forced by that dilemma to live in sin may well blame the Supreme Court of the United States, Justice Black, of course, dissenting.

These are but a few of the possible complications. If the revolt against Nevada becomes nationwide, chaos will be the result. South Carolina started the first Civil War in this country and it looks as though her sister might have started the second. I am glad that I am a bachelor, and neutral, like Belgium and Holland.

Why Not Worry?

"**W**HY WORRY?" THE optimists say. I say, "Why *not* worry?" Was there ever a time in the history of the world when there were such magnificent opportunities for fretting as there are today? Then why not take advantage of them?

Every woman owes it to herself to do a little worrying every day, just in case. Cross a bridge each day, even if it's only a culvert. When a real bridge comes along, you'll be better prepared to handle it. As a veteran bridge-crosser, trouble-borrower, and fretter, I want to set down here a few of the rules that have contributed to my success as a worrier.

First, it is important for the beginner to find out what type of worry suits his temperament. Don't get into the wrong school. Don't be a square worrier in a round dilemma. Try yourself out on a few sample worries, and then make up your mind.

Don't put off worrying. Don't say: "Well, I won't worry today. I'm having too much fun. I'll worry tomorrow." Tomorrow you may be having *more* fun.

Don't let anyone tell you you're too young to worry. It's never too early to start. Some off the most brilliant bridge-crossing of today is being done by fretters in their teens.

When you get a good worry, stick to it. At first you will be likely to tell yourself, "Now it's perfectly silly of me to be fuming about this thing, because it's only a trifle." That's not the spirit.

Don't pick a real worry if you can grab yourself an imaginary one. Real worries count for only half as much as imaginary ones. The worrier with the greatest collection of prematurely crossed bridges to her credit is the one to command respect.

Personally, I like to track down some absurd little tribulation that other worriers have snooted, nurse it along, and build it up until it is a fine, upstanding disaster and I am a wreck. It appeals to the creative artist in me to mail a letter and then start worrying over whether I put a stamp on it or addressed it correctly, until I have to hurry home and lie down with cold compresses on my brow.

By keeping a sharp eye out for the obscurely dismal trouble, you'll be surprised to discover what capital worrying you can extract from trifles that at first glance seem to offer no opportunities whatever. Have you, for instance, tried worrying about something tactless or silly you think you may have said to a friend? Properly handled, a thought like this can spoil your day beautifully. Or whether he has said something intended to hurt you? The field is unlimited. Everyone has a score of worries that a little diligence will uncover.

But I certainly do not wish to neglect the classic worries, the old reliable giants such as your health, your financial security, the fate of Europe, the younger generation and the going-to-the-dogs of America.

Do not neglect these old stand-bys. Devote some time to them every day, just to keep your hand in. What do you think would happen to Heifetz and Iturbi if they failed to practice a few hours a day?

The Fate of Civilization is like needlework. You can take it up and worry about it at odd moments. I myself worry about the Fate of Civilization ten times every morning near an open window, clad in just the lower part of my pajamas. It puts me in the right mood of dejection for breakfast, and if the coffee is inferior and I can find something like a piece of broken tumbler in the scrambled eggs, then my day is made, *i.e.*, spoiled.

Don't neglect your health. I mean, of course, don't neglect to worry about your health. You may think you are well now; but if you do, you are living in a fool's paradise, for the chances are you are coming down with something this very moment. You feel all right? Well, just read a few medical books. I guarantee you at least fifty symptoms. After that, rush to the nearest doctor. If he says you are sound as a bell, don't be discouraged. Rush to another doctor, and another, until you find one who knows his business and will assure you that you have defective tonsils, claustrophobia, a skippety heart, incipient mania, caries, migraine, mother fixation, asthma, nephritis, acute appendicitis or tic; choice of four.

If you can't worry about your own health, no matter how hard you try, there are always your family and friends. I know a woman who has worried steadily for nineteen years about her only son's health, without one single day's vacation. And what has been her reward for this devotion? The stubborn cub is in college at the moment, playing football in a disgusting state of health. He eats Welsh rabbit at three in the morning and goes without his rubbers in the most violent storms, with never a resulting pain or ache. How sharper than a serpent's tooth it is to have a thankless child!

Don't forget to worry about money, either. The technique is positively Grecian in its simplicity. People fall into just two classes: those who have money and those who have none. If you have none, all you have to do is worry about getting some. If you have lots, you worry for fear you may lose it.

To recapitulate: Pay no attention to those who tell you not to worry. If someone says to you, "There is absolutely no cause for alarm," flee his presence that instant and get yourself a cause for alarm. Let no day pass without crying over some spilt milk, if you have to spill it yourself. Always trouble trouble before it troubles you. A good attack is absolutely the best defense.

How to Change a Typewriter Ribbon

WHAT CHANCE OF survival in this machine age has a fellow to whom the slightest mechanical process is a mystery as deep as the secret of perpetual motion? I was wondering about this a little while ago when I was changing the ribbon on a typewriter; rather, just after I had kicked the typewriter from me with ribbon unchanged, and called for a machete with which to hack my way to safety through the tangle of typewriter ribbon that enmeshed me.

The book of instructions said to unwind some of the ribbon from the new spool and insert the ribbon into the slot in the ribbon spool cup. (Fig. 4.) Like a fool, I did. How was I to know? Then it said I was to turn the spool counter-clockwise, with slight downward pressure, until it was way down in proper position (top flange of spool about ⅛ inch above edge of spool cup). Then I had to look in the dictionary to find out what a flange was.

Then the book said I was to hold the empty spool in the left hand, tip the spool toward me so that the back of the hub was uppermost, place the loose end of the ribbon on the spool hub over the spear in the hub and hold the end of the ribbon tightly against the spool hub, with the index finger of the left hand, while pulling on the ribbon with the right hand until the spool hub spear pierces the ribbon about ½ inch from the end—see Fig. 5.

Fig. 5 was a picture of a man's thumb, so I thought, What would General MacArthur do in a fix like this? I decided that he would

71

push down in front over the front case base cleat, Fig. 1, until the front cleat latch snapped into latched position, so that's what I did. Then I pushed the front blase kate bleat; no, the front klase bate keat, but found that in so doing I was following the instructions for placing the typewriter in its case, having turned two pages of the instruction book in my excitement.

Returning to the instructions for changing the ribbon, I proceeded to crowd the lower or red edge of the ribbon down into the lower loop D of the vibrator as shown in Fig. 8, but was worried by the realization that I do not use a lower or red edge on my ribbon, preferring an all-black record ribbon. So I proceeded to manipulate the manual reverse lever by pulling it forward, see Fig. 7, income received from others, consisting of salaries, wages, fees, commissions, bonuses and other compensation for personal services. This brought me to the paper release lever, or total net short-term capital gain or loss, which I entered as item 1, page 1. Then I made sure to see that the coverplate latch lug, see Fig. 10, was snapped over the spring-board. Then the typewriter up and bit me. Naturally, I fought back.

I pulled the ribbon to the right and left to make sure it was properly threaded through the vibrator without twists or creases, see Fig. 9, and then I gave it a good swift kick, forgetting I was in bedroom slippers.

Then my aged relative came running upstairs, crying, "My goodness, such language! What in heaven's name is the matter?"

"See Fig. 8!" I roared, spitting several feet of typewriter ribbon at her.

The Wolf Sentence

THERE ARE PERSONS who have a gift for what may be called the wolf sentence in sheep's clothing. It is not double talk, exactly. It sounds innocent enough until you begin to think it over to find out what it means. Then it is apt to drive you loony, if you haven't enough strength of character to banish it from your mind.

The classic example is attributed to Mr. Dave Clark of Broadway who once, during an argument, is reported to have exclaimed, "Well, I may be wrong but I'm not far from it!"

It was Mr. Clark who almost unsettled the reason of the late Addison Mizner years ago. Mizner met Dave on Broadway and asked him about the merits of a new play that had just opened, and was it worth seeing.

"Oh, don't miss it if you can," urged Mr. Clark. Mr. Mizner thought that over for a few minutes and then ran screaming up Broadway.

A cherished friend of ours once glimpsed a lovely little mountain lake with evergreens growing down to its very water line.

"Look!" she exclaimed. "The lake comes right up to the shore!"

Another cherished friend recently said to us, "You know, I'm a split personality, all in one."

There is a lady in Hollywood, prominent in the life of the film capital, who is a never-ending source of pitfalls for her friends. Fascinated by the tales of this lady's mastery of the wolf sentence we

73

cautioned our Hollywood spies to put down every one of her mots and ship them to us pronto. Here is the cream of the lot:—

"There are lots of nice people in Hollywood—but not many."

"This is the best salad I ever put in my *whole* mouth."

"Oh, it was a heck of a party—everybody in the room was there."

"Is this room service? Well, please send me up some hot water juice."

"You can't make a cow's purse out of a sow's ear."

"Isn't he handsome—that other-looking fellow."

"A whole bunch of men came in surrounded by a little fellow in the middle."

"I've been standing at so many bars my elbows are bent."

"Waiters are much nicer than people."

"He tells a thing one morning and out the other."

"She had more money than she could afford."

"Two can live as cheap as one, but it costs them twice as much."

Then, although it is a simple case of malaprop and does not come in the category we have been discussing, there was the Hollywood producer who once told a friend of ours that his father was born in a town on one of the minor tribulations of the Rhine.

The Rape of the Grape

THE WIDOW PEETS'S annual war, known to tacticians as The Rape of the Grape, has ended as usual in victory for both sides. General Peets saved enough grapes for her winter supply of jell, with a few jars to spare for jell-mad neighbors. And the enemy was able to swipe enough of her grapes to satisfy his Grapes-raum, or annual September craving for grapes. Peace reigns now in the Peets garden and will do so until next September, since there are no apple or pear trees to tempt further aggression.

From long experience in these annual grape campaigns the Widow Peets has developed a technique in conducting her defense that might well arouse the respect of the best strategists. She knows that the enemy, being of an average age of ten, and male (therefore unhampered by skirts), is more mobile than she is. She knows also that she is better equipped by age, build and experience for psychological warfare than for counterattacks involving hot pursuit of the enemy. Like all good generals, she is a realist, and knows she is not going to be able to save all of her grapes. She is satisfied if she can keep her losses within a reasonable limit.

This does not mean that General Peets goes in for appeasement. She makes no gesture of that sort to the enemy. On the contrary she puts on a stern front to him which belies her great good nature and generosity. She knows also that an army travels on its stomach, even if that stomach be grape-lined. When her own source of supply is assured, she does not really mind if the enemy gets the surplus. Few commanders have as much consideration for the stomach of the enemy as General Peets shows.

This fall the enemy established himself in force on both flanks of the General's grape arbor. The Lincoln Avenue Dusters constructed the Burke Line, in the Burke back lot immediately to the east of the grape arbor. The Clark Street Terrors dug in down the alley, to the west. These forces were not allied. Oh, no, they operated independently and in competition. In fact, they have been known to highjack each other of valuable cargoes of grapes. Active raids on the General's arbor were confined almost entirely to after dark. The daylight hours were given to cautious reconnoitering expeditions, usually turned into disorderly retreat by the appearance of General Peets, with broom.

The General adopted a defense in depth. Threats of physical violence were found to have small effect on the enemy, whose shrewd intelligence service was aware that she had no intention of resorting to violence. Threats to tell the enemy's fathers or mothers had some effect at first, but diminished as the foe realized that she had no intention of doing that either. Threats to call the cops gave some pause, as the enemy remembered the time it set the field afire last spring and the cops really did show up.

If anyone was victorious it was Field Marshal Peets (whom we just promoted after tasting some of her grape jell). After deciding that the enemy had had enough grapes for his own good, she adopted a scorched-earth policy by going out with several dishpans and stripping the arbor of every last grape.

Pretty soon the savory aroma of victory permeated the neighborhood.

The Cliché Expert Testifies on War

Q: MR. ARBUTHNOT, if you are prepared, I should like today to go into the subject of the cliché as applied to war.

A: I am at your service, Mr. Smith.

Q: Thank you. Mr. Arbuthnot, what is war?

A: That depends on how you look at it.

Q: What do you mean by that?

A: It depends on whether you agree with Hitler or with General Sherman. Sherman thought that war was hell. Hitler thinks war is an ennobling experience in whose purifying fires the souls of men are cleansed and sanctified.

Q: What does war do?

A: War impends.

Q: You mean that Europe's fate—

A: Is hanging in the balance. I mean also that Europe is sitting on the top of a smoldering volcano. The international situation is grave.

Q: How do you know that the international situation is grave?

A: I have it on diplomatic authority—*high* diplomatic authority. The Quai d'Orsay is making no effort to conceal its anxiety. Likewise Downing Street.

Q: Which war is it that impends, Mr. Arbuthnot?

A: The war to end war.

Q: That being the general situation, how would you describe the present state of Europe?

Europe is an armed camp.

Q: How would you say it is armed?

A: Europe is armed to the teeth.

Q: That is to say, the nations are eager to go to war again.

A: You mean that they are eager to appeal to the sword. But you are wrong, Mr. Smith. The nations of Europe are not eager to appeal to the sword. They want peace. Or, as a cliché expert like myself would prefer to put it, they are sincerely desirous of living in amity and concord with their neighbors.

Q: Who says so?

A: Hitler. Mussolini. The Japs.

Q: Then why are they all arming to the teeth?

A: You mean why are they arraying themselves in the full panoply of war? It is because they *have* to go to war, Mr. Smith.

Q: Why do they have to go to war?

A: Sir, to avenge their national honor.

Q: What national honor?

A: Your Honor, must I answer that question?

THE COURT: I think not, on the ground that it might tend to incriminate and degrade friendly Powers.

A: You see, Mr. Smith, Hitler does not really want war. He simply wants Germany to have a place in the sun.

Q: Can't she get a place in the sun?

A: No.

Q: Why not?

A: Because the sun is too busy never setting on the British Empire.

Q: I see. But why did Mussolini attack Ethiopia?

A: Oh, but he didn't attack Ethiopia. Ethiopia affronted the national honor of Italy.

Q: When?

A: Forty years ago, at Aduwa. And Mussolini had to avenge Italy's national honor.

Q: How?

A: By bringing the blessings of civilization to Ethiopia.

Q: I see. How about Japan, Mr. Arbuthnot?

A: Japan wants peace with a burning passion, but she must fulfill her imperial destiny.

Q: How?

A: By bringing the blessings of civilization to China. And of course, in addition to avenging their national honor, the nations must expand.

Q: Why must they expand?

A: Because they have an excess of population.

Q: Why have they got an excess of population?

A: Because they must have plenty of males to fight the wars of expansion made necessary by the excess of population. Italy must expand. Germany must expand. Japan must expand. And Britain won't contract.

Q: Which results in?

A: Which results in what is technically known as a mad scramble for power.

Q: Mr. Arbuthnot, do you care to venture a guess at the future course of events in Europe, in your capacity as a cliché expert?

A: I will do so gladly. Eventually, there will be one too many affronts to national honor. Ultimatums will be issued, and apologies demanded. Representations will be made. There will be what I like to call warlike gestures. Diplomats will hurry to the Foreign Office, where lights will be seen burning far into the night. It will be an open secret that the situation is fraught with danger. The chancelleries of Europe will express grave concern for the balance of power. Responsibility for war will be placed on the shoulders of every nation by every other nation—placed *squarely*. Every effort will be made to avert an outbreak of hostilities and avoid a worldwide conflagration.

Q: How?

A: By mobilizing the armies and rushing troops to the frontier.

Q: Then what?

A: Then Armageddon. Cry havoc. Let loose the dogs of war. Unsheath the sword. The tramp of marching feet. The glint of bayonets. The serried ranks. Zero hour. Over the top. No Man's Land. Take no prisoners. Gas. Distant booming of guns. Seventy killed in air raid. Grim-visaged war in a world gone mad with blood lust. And the song of a lark at dawn in a wheatfield running red.

Q: Who do the actual fighting?

A: The flower of a nation's youth.

Q: What is the technical name for these young men?

A: Cannon fodder, or our brave boys.

Q: What do they do?

A: They leave home and fireside, factory and plough, to do their bit.

Q: How do they do their bit?

A: By giving their all. They make the supreme sacrifice. They die a hero's death.

Q: And their reward is—

A: They are buried with full military honors and are enshrined in the hearts of their countrymen.

Q: Mr. Arbuthnot, what was it the mother didn't do?

A: She didn't raise her boy to be a soldier.

Q: And the mother who didn't raise her boy to be a soldier turned out to be which mother?

A: The Gold Star mother.

Q: Now then, after the nations have been bled white, the countries laid waste, the cities reduced to ashes and the populations to starvation, the national honors avenged, the foe repelled, and in Flanders fields the poppies blow between the crosses row on row—what happens then?

A: The dove of peace makes its appearance. There are peace overtures.

Q: Why?

A: Because there never was a good war or a bad peace.

Q: What happens then?

A: Then there is the peace conference.

Q: What does the peace conference do?

A: It liberates the oppressed and downtrodden of all nations.

Q: Then what?

A: Then the nations start arming to the teeth to avenge the next affront to their national honor by means of the next war to end war.

Back to Normalcy

A CHEERFUL HARBINGER rang the doorbell the other day—the Fuller brush man. We gave him an even warmer greeting than we gave the first robin two months ago. We chose to regard the reappearance of the brush man as a good omen, an auspicious sign that normalcy is not too far away.

Our old Fuller brush man vanished soon after Pearl Harbor, along with automobiles, tires, tin containers, electric gadgets, Nylon stockings and double-breasted suits. Then, after an interval, a Fuller brush *woman* showed up. She was a friendly little body and did the best she could, but there was no blinking the fact that after all she was not the Fuller brush *man*. An agreeable substitute, but not the original. Then she disappeared, at about the time Scotch tape, tissue cleaners and ten-year-old Scotch went. Vanished into the WAVES, or WACS or SPARS.

Now, lint and dust may tremble, for the Fuller brush man is back. Not the same individual, but the same institution, which is what really matters.

That is the way it will be. At least, we hope so. One by one the old stand-bys reappearing in the wake of the pioneer brush man. Perhaps some day soon the doorbell will ring and the visitor will prove to be our old friend, the young man working his way through college by selling magazine subscriptions. Will the chatelaine give the lad the brush-off he sometimes got in the olden days? No indeed.

More likely he will be clasped to her bosom in a damp, tempestuous reunion. After him perhaps will come the lady selling greeting cards and stationery, and the Hoover automatic salesman, and the book agent. And the man asking respectfully if you'd like your lawn mower sharpened. (At the moment lawn mowers have to be transported to this potentate's lair, and he then tells you how rushed he is, but that he will do his best and try to give you back your machine by October.)

In the halcyon days that are sure to come, the housewife will have calls from glamorous creatures selling her, nay, begging her to buy, on the easiest possible terms, items whose names she has almost forgotten how to pronounce—electric toasters, ditto refrigerators, and washing machines. And lo, the radio repair man will be Johnny-on-the-spot to fix your radio a half hour after you summon him!

These old friends, the salesmen, will not get the bum's rush or have the door slammed in their faces as sometimes happened in the old days, especially when their doorbell ring summoned a testy housewife from her oven at a critical moment in the creation of a cake.

When they start ringing American doorbells again the boys will be lucky if they are not hauled inside by physical force and plunked down in front of a fatted calf, with all the fixin's.

A Needed Reform

IN THAT CALM and cheerful testament Irvin S. Cobb left behind him he touched courageously on points which have bothered a good many of us sinners. For one thing, Mr. Cobb spoke his mind firmly against pallbearers. This will add greatly to the debt of gratitude his friends owe his memory.

That lugubrious institution, the honorary pallbearer, is probably responsible for more casualties among our valued citizens than ever appear in any table of mortality statistics.

Naturally, when a man reaches the neighborhood of sixty his old friends begin to pack up, one by one, and leave for Home. He finds himself taking part oftener in processions to the cemetery. After a certain number of these ceremonies he begins to get low in his mind, quite naturally, and he starts wondering if his own number may not be up. If he is of a moody, brooding nature he may go home, make his will, and call the mortician. If he is robust and sanguine enough to throw off all this gloomy suggestion, like as not he catches pneumonia anyhow from standing bareheaded in the rain while an old friend, now safe from pneumonia, is borne out of the church.

The more noted the departed, the more honorary pallbearers he rates. It is not an uncommon sight in New York, when some eminent citizen passes on, to see thirty or forty distinguished judges, senators, doctors, actors, authors and other grandees lined up in escort, silk hats in hand. The politicians are usually in the majority at these macabre festivals. They seem to outlast their colleagues from the arts and professions. This is no doubt because politicians are tougher than any other form of human life to start with, and also because a politician instinctively holds more tenaciously to any job he gets, including that of being a human being.

Nobody quite knows who benefits by the appearance of forty silk-hatted gentlemen on these occasions. It cannot matter much to the departed unless, hovering over the scene, he gets a laugh when old Judge Cranberry (whom he never liked much anyhow) slips on the cathedral steps and nearly takes a header.

If I ever decide to leave any instructions I think I'll stipulate that if the family insists on pallbearers they spare my friends the dismal office and turn the job over to a posse of folks who never liked me, or vice versa. The task will give my haters much more pleasure than it would my friends, and it will probably make it easier to select an impressive group of pallbearers. In fact, there may be a waiting line. So let *them* stand bare-headed out in the cold, with the rain pelting down, catching pneumonia, while my friends are having a wake in some congenial tavern.

That's the way I'd like it to be. If the weather on the day of the funeral proves salubrious, I wish it postponed until there is a blizzard. If too many pallbearers volunteer under the terms outlined above, then I have no objection to giving encores until they are accommodated.

I have drawn up a list of twirps whom I wish to have as my pallbearers. Some I know. Some I have, thank God, never met. I would publish the list here except that it is too long.

The Cliché Expert Doesn't Feel Well

Q: MR. ARBUTHNOT, you are an expert in the use of the cliché as applied to matters of health and ill health, are you not?

A: I am.

Q: In that case, how do you feel?

A: Oh, fair to middling. I suppose I can't complain.

Q: You don't sound so awfully chipper.

A: What's the use of complaining? I hate people who are always telling their friends about their ailments. O-o-h!

Q: What's the matter?

A: My head. It's splitting. I've had one of my sick headaches all day long.

Q: One of your *sick* headaches, eh. What caused it?

A: I don't know. I haven't been feeling right lately. My stomach has been bothering me. My knee has been bothering me. My head has been bothering me. Yesterday I had one of my dizzy spells.

Q: Really? That's too bad.

A: I thought my time had come.

Q: What was it? Did something you ate disagree with you?

A: Nothing I eat ever agrees with me. But I mustn't talk about myself. You'll be thinking I'm a hypochondriac. You know the definition of a bore—a fellow who tells you how he feels when you ask him. . . . Oh, what was that?

Q: Just an auto backfiring. You're rather jumpy.

85

A: I'm nervous as a cat, you know. The least little thing upsets me. I'm just about two jumps ahead of a fit most of the time.

Q: I suppose you don't sleep well.

A: Why, I go to bed all tired out and then don't get a wink of sleep. Don't shut my eye all night long. Just lie there and toss. Least little thing wakens me. And when I get up in the morning I'm just as tired as when I went to bed. Just like a rag, no good all day.

Q: Have you taken anything?

A: I've taken everything but nothing seems to do me any good.

Q: Maybe you're coming down with a cold.

A: Oh, I always have a cold. I'm subject to colds.

Q: There's certainly quite a lot of 'em around.

A: You know, I'm supposed to say that. I'm the cliché expert around here, not you.

Q: I beg your pardon, Mr. Arbuthnot.

A: Quite all right. I was merely about to say that if anything's around I'll catch it. I always caught everything going. I was very delicate as a child. They had quite a time raising me.

Q: Really?

A: Yes, indeed. When I was ten years old the doctors gave me six months to live. Said they wouldn't give "That!" for my chances.

Q: Well, you fooled 'em.

A: Sometimes I wonder. O-o-h!

Q: What's the matter?

A: That stitch in my side. It's bothering me again.

Q: Maybe it's your appendix. Have you had it out?

A: Have I! I'll never forget that experience. They had to rush me to the hospital and operate immediately. The doctor said mine was the worst case he had seen in all his practice. He came twice a day for a week. I had a day and night nurse. They just took it in time.

Q: You neglected it, eh?

A: Oh, it doesn't pay to neglect your health, I always say. And I always say that if you've got your health you don't have to worry about money.

Q: How true.

A: O-o-o-h!

Q: Now what's the matter?

A: My back has gone back on me again. There's a crick in it.

Q: Why don't you see a doctor?

A: I've seen every one in town. I've been to the best specialists. None of them understands my case. They don't know what's the matter with me. They say "Cut down on your drinking and smoking, get plenty of rest, and don't worry." Don't worry, me eye! How's a person going to keep from worrying when his head—oh, but let's talk about something else except me. I don't want you to think I'm one of those people who are always talking about their bodily ailments and so on.

Q: Oh, do go on. I love to hear other people talk about their ailments.

A: You know this new doctor on Main Street?

Q: Yes. Quite a bright young fellow, they tell me.

A: Maybe so, but this is the experience I had with him. I went to see him the other day. I'd tried all the others, and thought I might as well try him, too. I told him how I was all run-down and he gave me a thorough going-over. And what do you think the young whippersnapper had the nerve to tell me?

Q: What?

A: He told me there wasn't a thing the matter with me. He said to me, "You think about yourself too much. What you need is something to occupy your mind. Why don't you take up golf?" Golf! With my heart!

Q: Oh, you have a bad heart, too?

A: Yes. A bum ticker. Doctors indeed!

Q: What about 'em?

A: They're never in when you want 'em.

Q: What else?

A: They're all specialists nowadays. Give me the old-fashioned family doctor. Imagine telling a man with a weak heart to take up golf.

Q: But, Mr. Arbuthnot, you look the picture of health to me.

A: Nonsense. I wouldn't want my worst enemy to go through what I've been through. You don't by any chance think I'm a hypochondriac, do you?

Q: Oh, no! No, no!

A: I don't talk about my health, do I?

Q: No, indeed. Far from it.

A: I mean to say, if you ask me how I am, I have to answer you, don't I? Well, I guess it's my turn to go in now. I think the doctor's ready for me.

Q: Heaven help him.

A: I beg your pardon.

Q: I didn't say a thing. Good-by, Mr. Arbuthnot.

A: Good day, son. O-o-oh, my back!

The Night the Old Nostalgia
Burned Down

My Own New York Childhood

WHEN I WAS a boy, Fourteenth Street was where Twenty-third Street is now, and Samuel J. Tilden and I used to play marbles on the lot where the Grand Opera House still stood. Governor Lovelace brought the first marble from England to this country on August 17, 1668, and gave it to my Great-Aunt Amelia van Santvoort, of whom he was enamored. She had several copies made, and Sam Tilden and I used to amuse ourselves with them.

I remember the Sunday afternoons when Governor Lovelace would come to tea at our house, although I could not have been much more than a tad at the time. I can hear the rich clanking of the silver harness as his magnificent equipage, with its twelve ebony outriders in cerise bombazine, rolled up to our house at No. 239 East 174th Street. I was the envy of all the kids on the block because I was allowed to sit in the carriage while the Governor went in to take tea with Great-Aunt Amelia. I always chose Ada Rehan to sit beside me. She was a little golden-haired thing at the time and none of us dreamed she would one day go out from East 174th Street and shoot President Garfield.

Great-Aunt Amelia was a dowager of the old school. You don't see many of her kind around New York today, probably because the old school was torn down a good many years ago; its site is now occupied by Central Park. People used to say that the Queen, as they called Great-Aunt Amelia, looked more like my Aunt Theodosia than my Aunt Theodosia did.

But Aunt Caroline was really the great lady of our family. I can still see her descending the staircase, dressed for the opera in silk hat, satin-lined cape, immaculate shirt, white tie, and that magnificent, purple-black beard.

"Well, boy!" she would boom at me. "Well!"

"Well, Aunt Caroline!" I would say, doing my best to boom back at her.

She would chuckle and say, "Boy, I like your spirit! Tell Grimson I said to add an extra tot of brandy to your bedtime milk."

Oh, those lollipops at Preem's, just around the corner from the corner! Mm-m-m, I can still taste them! After school, we kids would rush home and shout, "Ma, gimme a penny for a lollipop at Preem's, willya, Ma? Hey, Ma, willya?" Then we would go tease Jake Astor, the second-hand-fur dealer around the corner. I shall never forget the day Minnie Maddern Fiske swiped the mink pelt from Jake's cart and stuffed it under Bishop Potter's cope.

Miss Hattie Pumplebutt was our teacher at P.S. 67. She was a demure wisp of a woman, with white hair parted in the middle, pince-nez that were forever dropping off her nose, always some lacy collar high around her throat, and paper cuffs. We adored her. Every once in a while she would climb up on her desk, flap her arms, shout "Whee-e-e! I'm a bobolink!," and start crowing. Or she would take off suddenly and go skipping about the tops of our desks with a dexterity and sure-footedness truly marvellous in one of her age. When we grew old enough, we were told about Miss Pumplebutt. She took dope. Well, she made history and geography far more interesting than a lot of non-sniffing teachers I have known.

One day, Jim Fisk and I played hooky from school and went to the old Haymarket on Sixth Avenue, which was then between Fifth and Seventh. We had two beers apiece and thought we were quite men about town. I dared Jim to go over and shoot Stanford White, never dreaming the chump would do it. I didn't know he was loaded. I got Hail Columbia from Father for that escapade.

Father was very strict about the aristocratic old New York ritual of the Saturday-night bath. Every Saturday night at eight sharp we would line up: Father, Mother, Diamond Jim Brady; Mrs. Dalrymple, the housekeeper; Absentweather, the butler; Aggie, the second girl; Aggie, the third girl; Aggie, the fourth girl; and twelve of us youngsters, each one equipped with soap and a towel. At a command from Father, we would leave our mansion on East Thirtieth Street and proceed solemnly up Fifth Avenue in single file to the old reservoir, keeping a sharp eye out for Indians. Then, at a signal from Papa, in we'd go. Everyone who was anyone in New York in those days had his Saturday-night bath in the reservoir, and it was there that I first saw and fell in love with the little girl whom I later made Duchess of Marlborough.

My Grandmamma Satterthwaite was a remarkable old lady. At the age of eighty-seven she could skip rope four hundred and twenty-two consecutive times without stopping, and every boy on the block was madly in love with her. Then her father failed in the crash of '87 and in no time she was out of pigtails, had her hair up, and was quite the young lady. I never did hear what became of her.

It rather amuses me to hear the youngsters of today enthusing about the croissants, etc., at Spodetti's and the other fashionable Fifth Avenue patisseries. Why, they aren't a patch on Horan's!

Mike Horan's place was at Minetta Lane and Washington Mews, and I clearly remember my father telling a somewhat startled Walt Whitman that old Mike Horan could bend a banana in two—with his bare hands! But I never saw him do it. We kids used to stand in front of his shop for hours after school waiting for Mike to bend a banana, but he never did. I can still hear the cheerful clang of his hammer on the anvil and the acrid smell of burning hoofs from the Loveland Dance Palace, across the way on Delancey Street, which was then Grand. Then the Civil War came and the property of the Loyalists was confiscated. I still have some old Loyalist property I confiscated on that occasion. I use it for a paperweight. Old Gammer Wilberforce was a Loyalist. We used to chase her down the street, shouting "Tory!" at her. Then she would chase us up the street, shouting:

> "*Blaine, Blaine, James G. Blaine!*
> *Continental liar from the State of Maine!*"

or:

> "*Ma! Ma! Where's my Pa?*"
> "*Gone to the White House, ha, ha ha!*"

Of course, very few white people ever went to Chinatown in those days. It was not until the Honorah Totweiler case that people became aware of Chinatown. I venture to say that few persons today would recall Honorah Totweiler, yet in 1832 the Honorah Totweiler case was the sensation of the country. In one day the circulation of the elder James Gordon Bennett jumped seventy-four thousand as a result of the Totweiler case.

One sunny afternoon in the autumn of September 23, 1832, a lovely and innocent girl, twelfth of eighteen daughters of Isaac Totweiler, a mercer, and Sapphira, his wife, set out from her home in Washington Mews to return a cup of sugar—but let the elder Bennett tell the story:

> It is high time [Bennett wrote] that the people of these United States were awakened to the menace in which the old liberties for which our forefathers fought and bled, in buff and blue, by day and night, at Lexington and Concord, in '75 and '76, have been placed as a result of the waste, the orgy of spending, the deliberate falsifications, the betrayal of public trust, and the attempt to set up a bureaucratic and unconstitutional dictatorship, of the current Administration in Washington. Murphy must go, and Tammany with him!

After dinner on Sundays, my Grandpa Bemis would take a nap, with the *Times*, or something, thrown over his face to keep out the glare. If he was in a good humor when he awoke, he would take us youngsters up to Dick Canfield's to play games, but as he was never in a good humor when he awoke, we never went to Dick Canfield's to play games.

Sometimes, when we kids came home from school, Mrs. Rossiter, the housekeeper, would meet us in the hall and place a warning finger on her lips. We knew what that meant. We must be on our good behavior. The wealthy Mrs. Murgatroyd was calling on Mother. We would be ushered into the Presence, Mother would tell us to stop using our sleeves as a handkerchief, and then Mrs. Murgatroyd would laugh and say, "Oh, Annie, let the poor children alone. Sure, you're only young once." Then she would lift up her skirt to the knee, fish out a huge wallet from under her stocking, and give us each $2,000,000. We loved her. Not only did she have a pair of d——d shapely stems for an old lady her age, but she was reputed to be able to carry six schooners of beer in each hand.

I shall never forget the night of the fire. It was about three o'clock in the morning when it started, in an old distaff factory on West Twelfth Street. I was awakened by the crackling. I shivered, for my brother, as usual, had all the bedclothes, and there I was, with fully three inches of snow (one inch powder, two inches crust) on my bare back. The next morning there were seven feet of snow on West Twenty-seventh Street alone. You don't get that sort of winter nowadays. That was the winter the elder John D. Rockefeller was frozen over solid from November to May.

On Saturdays we used to go with Great-Aunt Tib to the Eden Musee to see the wax figure of Lillian Russell. There was a woman! They don't build girls like her nowadays. You can't get the material, and even if you could, the contractors and the plumbers would gyp you and substitute shoddy.

I was six when the riots occurred. No, I was *thirty*-six. I remember because it was the year of the famous Horace Greeley hoax, and I used to hear my parents laughing about it. It was commonly believed that Mark Twain was the perpetrator of the hoax, although Charles A. Dana insisted to his dying day that it was Lawrence Godkin. At any rate, the hoax, or "sell," originated one night at the Union League Club when Horace chanced to remark to Boss Tweed that his (Horace's) wife was entertaining that night. The town was agog for days, no one having the faintest notion that the story was not on the level. Greeley even threatened Berry Wall with a libel suit.

❖　❖　❖

Well, that was New York, the old New York, the New York of gaslit streets, and sparrows (and, of course, horses), and cobblestones. The newsboy rolled the *Youth's Companion* into a missile and threw it on your front stoop and the postmen wore uniforms of pink velvet and made a point of bringing everybody a letter every day.

Eheu, fugaces! —

The Education of a Ganymede

A NDREW CARNEGIE and I both went to work as young boys, though in different years, but Mr. Carnegie must have worked for some time before *he* earned fourteen dollars a day. I made that much right away. My first job was a honey and I wish I had it back, for I have never again had a cinch like it. I was pump boy in the betting ring at the Saratoga race track. My duty—nay, my pleasure—was to pump cups of cold water from a crystal spring and hand them to thirsty sports lovers—winners and losers alike. I first got the job when I was ten years old. Lillian Russell was forty-one that year but was probably not saying so publicly. I lug her name into this memoir because, having once served her with a cup of water, I consider myself entitled to reminisce about her.

The pump was popular with the thirsty sports lovers because of the sweet, pleasant quality of the water that gushed from it when urged by the pump boy's willing hand. Holiday merrymakers visited the pump in droves, especially on hot days, and showered small change on the boy in return for his cooling offices. The job was a bonanza, good for twelve or fourteen dollars on a warm Saturday. And in 1902 fourteen dollars amounted to exactly fourteen dollars.

The salary was princely and the hours were delightful even by today's standards. The pump boy worked only during August and then only in the afternoon. That left most of the summer free for play, swimming, berry picking, and general lallygagging, and for weeding

95

the vegetable garden, too, unless you gave the male parent the slip. I held the job of pump boy for several years, not because it was impossible to find another Ganymede with my skill and charm but because my father worked at the race track and was a crony of Reed Landers, the superintendent.

The nut for the pump enterprise was fifteen cents and was usually written off within ten minutes after the opening of business on the first day. The plant consisted of a cigar box to hold the tips, three tin cups to hold the water, and a bookmaker's stool on which to rest the cigar box and cups. And, of course, the pump and the pump boy, *ipso facto*. I got the cigar box free, courtesy of Mr. Winship, our grocer. The tin cups cost a nickel each at Woolworth's. I borrowed the stool from John G. Cavanagh, a friendly man who managed, or refereed, the betting ring. He was the only man I ever knew who had a train named for him, the Cavanagh Special, which made two trips a year—to Saratoga from New York at the opening of the August meeting and back to New York on Getaway Day.

Each day at the start of business, I placed three dimes in the cigar box, an ancient gambit suggested by my friend and mentor Paris Archer, who was in the Ganymede business, too, though not in competition with me. To be sure, this artful piece of psychology did not always hypnotize the customers into dropping dimes into the box, but it probably did have a salutary effect in warding off pennies, a lowly form of specie unworthy of the attention of an apprentice tycoon. The ruse is still in vogue in theatre and night-club checkrooms, though the Turpins and Messalinas who run these modern cesspools of avarice would scorn to use dimes as bait.

I got so I could tell from a customer's approach what his luck had been. If a man came up jovially, called me Bub or Sonny, joshed me about the scads of money I must make, declared the water marvellous, and tossed a dime or even a quarter into the cigar box, I knew *that* man's horse had taken the dust of no rival. If the customer was preoccupied and brooding, and left a nickel or nothing, I gathered he had not been as clairvoyant as he could have wished, and I was glad to slake his thirst gratis, having no choice but to do so anyhow. Thus at a tender age did I acquire that shrewd insight into human nature which forsook me soon afterward.

There was one customer of whom I grew especially fond. He was a big, ruddy, friendly man; he always left a tip and usually stopped for a chat, and he did not patronize or talk down to a boy, as adults usually do. One day at the close of the meeting, I saw that my favorite customer was not his wonted genial self. Something was wrong. I soon found out what. He took me aside, confided that he was broke, and had exhausted all possible touches, and asked if I would lend him fifteen dollars to get back to New York. I felt honored. It was an accolade to have a man of the world put the bee on me, just as though I were another man of the world. I gladly handed over the fifteen dollars. If you think a disillusioning experience followed, it is my pleasant duty to disillusion you. A money order for the fifteen dollars reached me within the week. Through *this* experience I acquired that faith in the essential goodness of human nature which has been as a millstone around my neck ever since.

One opening day, I started in to the race track to assume my post for the season. I wore no employees' badge, because I had none; it was not thought necessary to dignify the pump boy with a badge. A Pinkerton at the gate stopped me and asked where I thought I was going, and wouldn't believe me when I told him. He was growing rather tiresome about the matter when a small, quick man with sideburns came along and asked what the trouble was.

The Pinkerton grew suddenly respectful. "Why, sir, this boy says he works inside, but he ain't got any badge. I figgered he's just tryin' to sneak in."

"You did, did you!" snapped the little man. "Well, you're wrong. He's the pump boy. Come along, boy."

He trotted off and I trotted off at his side, first casting a sneer of triumph at the discomfited lackey. We continued to trot along until, with a sort of bustling kindness, the little man deposited me safely at the pump. Paris Archer was overwhelmed when he saw my escort, and I was curious to know who this man was who could overawe even a Pinkerton. I asked Paris.

"He! Why, boy, he Mistah Pinkerton in pusson! He the boss man."

The boss was aware of so insignificant a cog as the pump boy, but the underling was not. There must have been a lesson here.

Paris Archer was an important factor in the education of the pump boy. He was a man of the world of considerable dash and élan, and, it may safely be added, no little savoir-faire. His complexion was a rich chocolate. Everything about him was rich. His raiment was rich. He had a rich laugh. When he laughed, a magnificent array of gleaming teeth was revealed, as far back as the eye could see, and when Paris laughed, the eye could *see!* It was his function to pass among the bookmakers with a pail of cold water, crying, "Watah, boss! Watah on de line, boss!" For thus saving Eddie Burke, Joe Ullman, Johnny Walters, and other bookmakers of that day from dehydration, Paris collected a daily cash compliment from each book. I imagine he had a very good thing of it.

A dapper man came to the pump one day. He wore such an air of quiet magnificence that I assumed he must be a visiting duke, or at least one of the Vanderbilts, with whom Saratoga teemed in those days. I asked Paris who he was.

"Big man," said Paris. "Ve'y impo'tant fashion plate name o' Be'y Wall."

I read the newspapers, and knew that Berry Wall was just about all ten of the best-dressed men of the day. Yet it seemed to my possibly biassed eye that Paris had it over Berry as a fashion plate. Paris was more dramatic. He was partial to silk shirts in solid colors like pink, and he usually wore a large diamond in his shirt front. To be sure, the jewel was not in the money with the traffic signals James Buchanan Brady wore in lieu of shirt studs, but still it was potent. If you got its full effect square in the eye on a sunny day, you couldn't see well for several moments. I thought Mr. Archer's haberdashery struck just the right note between the relative conservatism of Mr. Wall and the barbaric splendor of Diamond Jim.

The pump job was made to order for a Horatio Alger plot—the innocent tad plumped into the middle of a race-track betting ring. Would virtue triumph? Would the little man resist the temptation to gamble? Or would he take the primrose path, squander the contents of the cigar box on the ponies, and then reel home and strike his aged mother? My mother was not aged at that time and would have given an excellent account of herself in a passage with a refractory scion. Besides, I really could not see that a career as a plunger had much to offer. The lesson of my friend who had to borrow fifteen dollars from me to get back to New York was not lost on my budding comprehension. Anyhow, my father had the betting concession in our family. He was well nigh infallible at picking horses that finished fourth or later. I think what he sought to do was to smash the record of Pittsburgh Phil, a noted plunger of the day, who made a fortune of two millions playing the horses. My father tried valiantly to wrest Pittsburgh Phil's title from him but failed to do so by the two millions, plus many additional thousands. Yet he had an awfully good time failing, and was still happily at it when he was taken from this life, at eighty. There is a lesson here, too, but I don't think Horatio Alger would approve it.

I was more interested in sport for sport's sake than I was in betting, and had, in fact, only recently given up a sketchy dream of becoming a jockey, like Lester and Johnny Reiff, two young riders who had come to our house occasionally before they went abroad and became famous in England. (Lester won the Epsom Derby in 1901 and Johnny won it in 1907—with, of course, the aid of the two horses involved.) I gave up wanting to be a jockey one day when a character called Dynamite, a groom in the stable of a Mr. Ralph Black, put me on a thoroughbred, off whose back I fell shortly afterward, on my head. After that, I wanted to be an actor, not because of the concussion but because about that time I discovered the fascinating theatrical section of the *Morning Telegraph*, an organ of public opinion my father studied each day as part of his campaign to discomfit Pittsburgh Phil.

One afternoon, a man came to the pump and said, "Boy, take a cup of that spring water to Miss Lillian Russell, in Box So-and-So." It was as if Jupiter had said, "Boy, fetch a cup of nectar to Venus, over yonder on Cloud 27." I had often sneaked from my post at the pump out to the grandstand lawn to gaze up at the box where this fabled matron queened it. Her picture had the place of honor in my cigarette-card collection of stage favorites, outranking Maxine Elliott, Lotta Faust, and Frankie Bailey. But this was the first time she had ever asked to meet me.

Leaving the mortal customers to pump their own refreshment or go thirsty, I filled one of the tin chalices and bore it carefully up the grandstand stairway to Miss Russell's box.

As usual, there was a Pinkerton on guard at the top of the stairway. He stopped me. "Where you goin' with that?" he said.

"It's spring water for Miss Russell. She sent for it."

"Go back and bring it in a *glass*. Miss Russell don't want to drink out of no tin cup," said Mr. Pumblechook severely.

"Yes, she does," chimed a silvery voice. "Let the little boy come here."

A lot has been written about the charms of Lillian Russell, and none of it has been exaggerated. Each afternoon during the races, she sat in that front-tier box, regal but never haughty, generously allowing one and all to bask in the refulgence of her opulent, peaches-and-cream perfection. There was plenty of her, all top quality, and you felt sure that never in her life had this placid Aphrodite denied herself a broiled lobster with butter sauce, or a second helping of creamed potatoes. She reached for the cup, and drank. "My, it's good!" she said. "Thank you, little boy." The famed dimples did their devastating best. "Tastes better out of a tin cup, too."

For the second time, I had triumphed over a Pinkerton, and this, mind you, before my life had seen a baker's dozen summers.

The silvery voice chimed another thanks and the queen graciously carried out this happy color scheme by handing me a silvery tip of a half dollar. I daresay nothing like that happened to Andy Carnegie when he was bobbin boy in a cotton mill.

Close as was my friendship with Lillian Russell, I must admit with envy that a fellow-Saratogian of that day was even better acquainted with her. Master Charles Brackett, a schoolmate of mine, had the undeserved good fortune to live next door to the house Miss Russell leased annually for her Saratoga visit. Each evening, she dressed to go to Canfield's for fish and chips. Since her house was on a secluded avenue, her maid sometimes forgot or neglected to pull down the shades of the boudoir. I have heard Mr. Brackett tell that the tug of war to get the diva into her corset, with the maid hauling away like a Volga boatman and L. R. clutching the bedpost, was a wondrous and awe-inspiring spectacle. I presume Mr. Brackett, then as now an honorable gentleman, spoke from hearsay.

At the close of business each afternoon, I would clank home, soggy but wealthy, every pocket bulging with nickels and dimes and occasional quarters and, alas, occasional pennies. My mother and I would count the day's take and divide it into three parts. One pile was earmarked to buy my school clothes and winter haberdashery. A reasonable sum was appropriated to enable me to maintain my standing as a man-about-town and rakehell in the ice-cream parlors, nickelodeons, and penny arcades of summer Saratoga. The third share I donated as my contribution to the Sullivan grocery-and-coal fund.

Each June for six years, I went with hope and trepidation to Mr. Landers to ask for the job at the pump, and each June that benevolent man, after pretending to ponder the matter, gave it to me. Then the June came when Mr. Landers winced slightly at a lately acquired croak in my voice, and he asked if I didn't think it time a smaller boy had a whack at the pump job. I had been expecting this. I had to agree. So that August the pump went to a smaller neighbor. I became pump boy emeritus and worked that summer pasting labels on spring-water bottles, at seven dollars a week. In the nineteen-twenties, I was able to feel more sympathy than most for those grand dukes who, fresh from the emoluments of the Czar's court, had to take jobs as carriage starters.

The bookmaker of yore, with his stool and slate, has long since given place to pari-mutuels. A storeroom occupies the spot at the Saratoga race track where the pump once splashed. There have also been extensive changes in the pump boy. His advice to all men of ten is: Do not start at the top and work your way down, as he did. Be more like Andrew Carnegie.

An Old Grad Remembers

(Warning—The following will be incomprehensible to anyone who never went to Cornell University)

WHEN I WAS a freshman at Ithaca the University was down where the town is now and Ithaca was up on the hill by Bailey Hall. It was toward the close of a particularly frolicsome spring day that the positions were reversed. The Board of Trustees, once the shift had been made, never bothered to remedy it. "Laissez faire!" counselled a trustee who had majored in French.

Hiram Corson, Rym Berry, Goldwin Smith and myself comprised the Varsity crew that year, each man rowing four oars. There were giants in those days. Pearl White was the coxswain of our crew. Pearl White is not to be confused with E. B. (Andy) White, former editor of the *Sun*. Pearl was fuller around here, and here, and Andy wore suspenders. Ah, there were Pearl Whites in those days!

I'm afraid you lads will rue having started an old grad on these memories, but perhaps you will bear with me for a moment, or a week, for the sake of Auld Lang Syne, and the Annex, and Proctor Twesten, and Tar Young, and the short line to Auburn, and those trips up Buffalo hill after missing the jag car. (Buffalo Street ran UP hill in those days.)

I shall never forget the September afternoon I arrived in Ithaca. The seniors were wearing their blazers and the sophomores had just finished Senior Singing over by Goldwin Smith. Ah, there were sophomores in those days! You don't get sophomores like that nowadays. Can't get the stuff.

On a crisp autumn afternoon there was a tang to the air in the gymnasium that somehow made a fellow feel lucky to be alive. The good old Lyceum Theatre was still in existence, and Count Rogalsky and Lew Durland stood then at the northwest corner of State and Aurora. What times we students used to have in the "pit" at the Lyceum; carefree nights in the wonderful world of make-believe, nights which for many of us were our first taste of the drama. It was at the Lyceum I first saw Sothern and Marlowe in "Macbeth," and Sothern and Marlowe in "Floradora," and Marlowe and Sothern in "Juliet and Romeo." You don't see tap dancing like that any more.

I recall, too, those wonderful parties at the Dutch after the theatre, when Lillian Russell, or Lotta Faust, or Helena Modjeska, or some other reigning belle of showdom would come to town. We always drank champagne from the star's slipper, or if we happened to be extra thirsty, from one of the football captain's goloshes.

Where are the golden lads who were regulars at those gay suppers? David Starr Jordan never missed, and neither did dear old Professor Walter Heasley. Leroy P. Ward, Kid Kugler and "Steve" Stevenson were always present, and so was Dr. Hu Shih. Gesundheit! and dear old Professor Bishop, at that time doyen of the Department of Plant Pathology, whom we students, with that unerring instinct of the undergrad for pinning *le nicknom juste* on the faculty, always called "Morris G." But not to his face, you may be sure. Then there was dear old Raymond Howes, curator of the William Hazlitt Upson Numismatic Collection, and William Hazlitt Upson, at that time Raymond Howes Professor of Ornithology.

Will I ever forget the great revolt when the "frosh," as Professor George Lincoln Burr so happily dubbed them, refused to wear the traditional cap? Sure I will.

One of my first and most lasting friendships at Cornell was with a Jacob Gould Schurman who was President of the University. I would meet Dr. Schurman on the campus, tip my hat and say "Good morning, sir" and Dr. Schurman would return my greeting pleasantly. How I used to look forward to those bull sessions with J.G.!

Dear old Sage choir! I always thought it rather a pity that in the middle of a cantata one Sunday, Dr. Henry Ward Beecher suddenly turned a tommy gun on the choir and liquidated the entire mass of nightingales, save for one mezzo-soprano, a lady Vet student who, having heard of the good dominie's unpredictability, had taken the precaution to wear a surplice of chain mail. It was the first machine gun we fellows had ever seen and I recall how we crowded around Dr. Beecher after the massacre, plying him with questions about the new-fangled gadget and entreating him to let us try it out on the Dekes.

I remember those absurd things we used to eat at the Co-op in Morrill Hall between classes. They were called Wilbur Buds and, by Jove, they *looked* like Wilbur Buds, but yum, how good they used to taste. Good old Wilbur Buds. I suppose they have all been eaten.

Final examinations! What larks they were! Much more fun than the prelims, where the instructors served only soft drinks and buns, and never would slip us the answers. Does one ever, one wonders, quite forget the girl one took to one's first prelim?

What a fine body of men there was at Cornell in those days! In my class, for instance, all the men were over seven feet tall with the exceptions of John Wilkes Booth, Benjamin Ide Wheeler and myself. Only the weaklings of the class were allowed to play football. It would not have been fair to the other colleges to use our healthier classmates. Leon Czolgosz was voted Best Dresser of my class. It was Leon who later caused not a few raised eyebrows by shooting President McKinley, though the two had been excellent friends in college.

Percy Field on the afternoon of a big game. The stands are jammed, the October air bracing and the sun is getting low in, if my memory serves, the West. It is the last minute of the last quarter and the bases are full. Dartmouth, on our one-yard line, has taken two of our pawns and a castle. A groan from the crowd! Then, just as all seems lost, a flash of red and white oars in the distance, and we know that Pop Courtney has done it again at Poughkeepsie! What a roar goes up from that crowd! I can hear it now, or is that my blood pressure?

They were wonderful days. *Eheu*, as Bull Durham used to say, *fugaces*. Beer was a nickel a seidel at Hi Henry's. John Paul Jones had just introduced the principle of jet propulsion into the mile run. With Carl Hallock in the White House under the name of Rutherford B. Hayes, the country was happy and prosperous. Little did we dream that two wars and the Alumni Fund were just around the corner.

Ah, well. Those were the days. Excuse my emotion, but I wouldn't exchange the memory of those four wonderful years at Hobart for all the wealth of the Indies.

The Cliché Expert Testifies
on Baseball

Q: MR. ARBUTHNOT, you state that your grandmother has passed away and you would like to have the afternoon off to go to her funeral.

A: That is correct.

Q: You are an expert in the clichés of baseball—right?

A: I pride myself on being well versed in the stereotypes of our national pastime.

Q: Well, we'll test you. Who plays baseball?

A: Big-league baseball is customarily played by brilliant outfielders, veteran hurlers, powerful sluggers, knuckle-ball artists, towering first basemen, key moundsmen, fleet base runners, ace southpaws, scrappy little shortstops, sensational war vets, ex-college stars, relief artists, rifle-armed twirlers, dependable mainstays, doughty right-handers, streamlined backstops, power-hitting batsmen, redoubtable infielders, erstwhile Dodgers, veteran sparkplugs, sterling moundsmen, aging twirlers, and rookie sensations.

Q: What other names are rookie sensations known by?

A: They are also known as aspiring rookies, sensational newcomers, promising freshmen, ex-sandlotters, highly touted striplings, and youngsters who will bear watching.

Q: What's the manager of a baseball team called?

A: A veteran pilot. Or youthful pilot. But he doesn't manage the team.

Q: No? What does he do?

A: He guides its destinies.

Q: How?

A: By the use of managerial strategy.

Q: Mr. Arbuthnot, please describe the average major-league-baseball athlete.

A: Well he comes in three sizes, or types. The first type is tall, slim, lean, towering, rangy, huge, husky, big, strapping, sturdy, handsome, powerful, lanky, rawboned, and rugged.

Q: Quite a hunk of athlete.

A: Well, those are the adjectives usage requires for the description of the Type One, or Ted Williams, ballplayer.

Q: What is Type Two like?

A: He is chunky or stocky—that is to say, Yogi Berra.

Q: And the third?

A: The third type is elongated and does not walk. He is Ol' Satchmo, or Satchel Paige.

Q: What do you mean Satchmo doesn't walk?

A: Not in the sports pages, he doesn't. He ambles.

Q: You mentioned a hurler, Mr. Arbuthnot. What is a hurler?

A: A hurler is a twirler.

Q: Well, what is a twirler?

A: A twirler is a flinger, a tosser. He's a moundsman.

Q: Moundsman?

A: Yes. He officiates on the mound. When the veteran pilot tells a hurler he is to twirl on a given day, that is a mound assignment, and the hurler who has been told to twirl is the mound nominee for that game.

Q: You mean he pitches?

A: That is right. You have cut the Gordian knot.

Q: What's the pitcher for the other team called?

A: He is the mound adversary, or mound opponent, of the mound nominee. That makes them rival hurlers, or twirlers. They face each other and have a mound duel, or pitchers' battle.

Q: Who wins?

A: The mound victor wins, and as a result he is a mound ace, or ace moundsman. He excels on the mound, or stars on it. He and the other moundsmen on his team are the mound corps.

Q:　What happens to the mound nominee who loses the mound duel?

A:　He is driven off the mound.

Q:　What do you mean by that?

A:　He's yanked. He's knocked out of the box.

Q:　What's the box?

A:　The box is the mound.

Q:　I see. Why does the losing moundsman lose?

A:　Because he issues, grants, yields, allows, or permits too many hits or walks, or both.

Q:　A bit on the freehanded side, eh? Where does the mound victor go if he pitches the entire game?

A:　He goes all the way.

Q:　And how does the mound adversary who has been knocked out of the box explain his being driven off the mound?

A:　He says, *"I had trouble with my control,"* or *"My curve wasn't working,"* or *"I just didn't have anything today."*

Q:　What happens if a mound ace issues, grants, yields, allows, or permits too many hits and walks?

A:　In that case, sooner or later, rumors are rife. Either that or they are rampant.

Q:　Rife where?

A:　In the front office.

Q:　What's that?

A:　That's the place where baseball's biggies—also known as baseball moguls—do their asking.

Q:　What do they ask for?

A:　Waivers on erratic southpaw.

Q:　What are these baseball biggies further known as?

A:　They are known as the Shrewd Mahatma or as Horace Stoneham, but if they wear their shirt open at the neck they are known as Bill Veeck.

Q:　What do baseball biggies do when they are not asking for waivers?

A:　They count the gate receipts, buy promising rookies, sell aging twirlers, and stand loyally by Manager Durocher.

Q:　And what does Manager Durocher do?

A: He guides the destinies of the Giants and precipitates arguments with the men in blue.

Q: What men in blue?

A: The umpires, or arbiters.

Q: What kind of arguments does Durocher precipitate?

A: Heated arguments.

Q: And the men in blue do what to him and other players who
precipitate heated arguments?

A: They send, relegate, banish, or thumb them to the showers.

Q: Mr. Arbuthnot, how do you, as a cliché expert, refer to first
base?

A: First base is the initial sack.

Q: And second base?

A: The keystone sack.

Q: What's third base called?

A: The hot corner. The first inning is the initial frame, and an
inning without runs is a scoreless stanza.

Q: What is one run known as?

A: A lone run, but four runs are known as a quartet of tallies.

Q: What is a baseball?

A: The pill, the horsehide, the old apple, or the sphere.

Q: And what's a bat?

A: The bat is the willow, or the wagon tongue, or the piece of
lumber. In the hands of a mighty batsman, it is the mighty bludgeon.

Q: What does a mighty batsman do?

A: He amasses runs. He connects with the old apple. He raps
'em out and he pounds 'em out. He belts 'em and he clouts
'em.

Q: Clouts what?

A: Circuit clouts.

Q: What are they?

A: Home runs. Know what the mighty batsman does to the
mighty bludgeon?

Q: No. What?

A: He wields it. Know what kind of orgies he fancies?

Q: What kind?

A: Batting orgies. Slugfests. That's why his team pins.

Q: Pins what?

A: All its hopes on him.

Q: Mr. Arbuthnot, what is a runner guilty of when he steals home?

A: A plate theft.

Q: And how many kinds of baseball games are there?

A: Five main classifications: scheduled tussles, crucial contests, pivotal games, drab frays, and arc-light tussles.

Q: And what does the team that wins—

A: Sir, a baseball team never wins. It scores a victory, or gains one, or chalks one up. Or it snatches.

Q: Snatches what?

A: Victory from the jaws of defeat.

Q: How?

A: By a ninth-inning rally.

Q: I see. Well, what do the teams that chalk up victories do to the teams that lose?

A: They nip, top, wallop, trounce, rout, down, subdue, smash, drub, paste, trip, crush, curb, whitewash, erase, bop, slam, batter, check, hammer, pop, wham, clout, and blank the visitors. Or they zero them.

Q: Gracious sakes! Now I know why ballplayers are old at thirty-five.

A: Oh, that isn't the half of it. They do other things to the visitors.

Q: Is it possible?

A: Certainly. They jolt them, or deal them a jolt. They also halt, sock, thump, larrup, vanquish, flatten, scalp, shellac, blast, slaughter, K.O., mow down, topple, whack, pound, rap, sink, baffle, thwart, foil, maul, and nick.

Q: Do the losers do anything at all to the victors?

A: Yes. They bow to the victors. And they taste.

Q: Taste what?

A: Defeat. They trail. They take a drubbing, pasting, or shellacking. They are in the cellar.

Q: What about the victors?

A: They loom as flag contenders. They're in the first division.

Q: Mr. Arbuthnot, what is the first sign of spring?

A: Well, a robin, of course.

Q: Yes, but I'm thinking of our subject here. How about when the ballplayers go south for spring training?

A: Ballplayers don't go south for spring training.

Q: Why, they do!

A: They do *not*. They wend their way southward.

Q: Oh, I see. Well, do all ballplayers wend their way southward?

A: No. One remains at home.

Q: Who is he?

A: The lone holdout.

Q: Why does the lone holdout remain at home?

A: He refuses to ink pact.

Q: What do you mean by that?

A: He won't affix his Hancock to his contract.

Q: Why not?

A: He demands a pay hike, or salary boost.

Q: From whom?

A: From baseball's biggies.

Q: And what do baseball's biggies do to the lone holdout?

A: They attempt to lure him back into the fold.

Q: How?

A: By offering him new contract.

Q: What does lone holdout do then?

A: He weighs offer. If he doesn't like it, he balks at terms. If he does like it, he inks pact and gets pay hike.

Q: How much pay hike?

A: An undisclosed amount in excess of.

Q: That makes him what?

A: One of the highest-paid baseball stars in the annals of the game, barring Ruth.

Q: What if baseball's biggies won't give lone holdout pay hike?

A: In that case, lone holdout takes pay cut, old salary, or job in filling station in home town.

Q: Now, when baseball players reach the spring training camp and put on their uniforms—

A: May I correct you again, sir? Baseball players do not put on uniforms. They don them.

Q: I see. What for?

A: For a practice session or strenuous workout.

Q: And why must they have a strenuous workout?

A: Because they must shed the winter's accumulation of excess avoirdupois.

Q: You mean they must lose weight?

A: You put it in a nutshell. They must be streamlined, so they plunge.

Q: Plunge into what?

A: Into serious training.

Q: Can't get into serious training except by plunging, eh?

A: No. Protocol requires that they plunge. Training season gets under way in Grapefruit and Citrus Leagues. Casey Stengel bars night life.

Q: Mr. Arbuthnot, what is the opening game of the season called?

A: Let me see-e-e. It's on the tip of my tongue. Isn't that aggravating? Ah, I have it—the opener! At the opener, fifty-two thousand two hundred and ninety-three fans watch Giants bow to Dodgers.

Q: What do those fifty-two thousand two hundred and ninety-three fans constitute?

A: They constitute fandom.

Q: And how do they get into the ballpark?

A: They click through the turnstiles.

Q: Now then, Mr. Arbuthnot, the climax of the baseball season is the World Series, is it not?

A: That's right.

Q: And what is the World Series called?

A: It's the fall classic, or crucial contest, also known as the fray, the epic struggle, and the Homeric struggle. It is part of the American scene, like ham and eggs or pumpkin pie. It's a colorful event.

Q: What is it packed with?

A: Thrills. Drama.

Q: What kind of drama?

A: Sheer or tense.

Q: Why does it have to be packed with thrills and drama?

A: Because if it isn't, it becomes drab fray.

Q: Where does the fall classic take place?

A: In a vast municipal stadium or huge ballpark.

Q: And the city in which the fall classic is held is what?

A: The city is baseball mad.

Q: And the hotels?

A: The hotels are jammed. Rooms are at a premium.

Q: Tickets, also, I presume.

A: Tickets? If you mean the cards of admission to the fall classic, they are referred to as elusive Series ducats, and they *are* at a premium, though I would prefer to say that they are scarcer than the proverbial hen's teeth.

Q: Who attends the Series?

A: A milling throng, or great outpouring of fans.

Q: What does the great outpouring of fans do?

A: It storms the portals and, of course, clicks through the turnstiles.

Q: Causing what?

A: Causing attendance records to go by the board. Stands fill early.

Q: What else does the crowd do?

A: It yells itself hoarse. Pent-up emotions are released. It rides the men in blue.

Q: What makes a baseball biggie unhappy on the morning of a Series tussle?

A: Leaden skies.

Q: Who is to blame for leaden skies?

A: A character known to the scribes as Jupiter Pluvius, or Jupe.

Q: What does rain dampen?

A: The ardor of the fans.

Q: If the weather clears, who gets credit for that?

A: Another character, known as Old Sol.

Q: Now, the team that wins the Series—

A: Again, I'm sorry to correct you, sir. A team does not win a Series. It wraps it up. It clinches it.

Q: Well, then what?

A: Then the newly crowned champions repair to their locker room.

Q: What reigns in that locker room?

A: Pandemonium, bedlam, and joy.

Q: Expressed how?

A: By lifting youthful pilot, or his equivalent, to the shoulders of his teammates.

Q: In the locker room of the losers, what is as thick as a day in — I mean so thick you could cut it with a knife?

A: Gloom. The losers are devoid.

Q: Devoid of what?

A: Animation.

Q: Why?

A: Because they came apart at the seams in the pivotal tussle.

Q: What happens to the newly crowned champions later?

A: They are hailed, acclaimed, and fêted. They receive mighty ovations, boisterous demonstrations, and thunderous welcomes.

Q: And when those are over?

A: They split the Series purse and go hunting.

Q: Mr. Arbuthnot, if a powerful slugger or mighty batsman wields a mighty bludgeon to such effect that he piles up a record number of circuit clouts, what does that make him?

A: That is very apt to make him most valuable player of the year.

Q: And that?

A: That makes the kids of America look up to him as their hero.

Q: If most valuable player of the year continues the batting orgies that make the kids of America worship him, what then?

A: Then he becomes one of Baseball's Immortals. He is enshrined in Baseball's Hall of Fame.

Q: And after that?

A: Someday he retires and becomes veteran scout, or veteran coach, or veteran pilot. Or sports broadcaster.

Q: And then?

A: Well, eventually a memorial plaque is unveiled to him at the opener.

Q: Thank you, Mr. Arbuthnot. You have been most helpful. I won't detain you any longer, and I hope your grandmother's funeral this afternoon is a tense drama packed with thrills.

A: Thanks a lot. Goodbye now.

Q: Hold on a moment, Mr. Arbuthnot. Just for my own curiosity — couldn't you have said "thanks" and "goodbye" and let it go at that, without adding that "lot" and "now" malarkey?

A: I could have, but it would have cost me my title as a cliché expert.

A Watched Proverb Butters
No Parsnips

THE TRICK IN proverb quoting is simple. Pick a proverb that brings out your adversary's weakness, or makes him think he has a weakness, and shoot it at him before he has a chance to shoot one at you. This gives you the upper hand right away. Well begun is half done.

I suspect most proverbs were thought up by people who thought too well of themselves and too little of their fellow men, especially if the fellow men were children. Half our stock of maxims is designed to quell children. When I was a cub, some elder would tell me every so often, with a trace of reproach in his voice, that handsome is as handsome does. I was not handsome. I knew it, and I suspected that elders who told me handsome was as handsome did were taking cracks at my freckles. Ripened in years as I now am, I know that handsome doesn't necessarily do as handsome is, or isn't necessarily is as handsome does. Therefore, I never tell children that it is as it does, meaning handsome. I never tell anybody that; I never quote any maxim or proverb at youth or adult. People who live in glass houses.

Children, of course, are sitting ducks for proverbs. They are too young to know that proverbs are not always 100 per cent right. They, the proverbs, would like to give you that impression, however. They (still the proverbs) have been hanging around in the language

for so long that, by squatter sovereignty, they claim to be infallible.
But they are not infallible. Two heads better than one? Not on the
same person. Close examination would reveal similar leaks in other
maxims.

You may bear the scars of handsome is as handsome does or of
some other proverb. I know a girl who says she still feels the effects
of the one about a stitch in time saving nine. She tried such a stitch
often, she says, but never saved nine, or even two. Her fingers were
mainly thumbs when it came to needlework and every time she
tried to save nine stitches in time, the thimble fell off her finger, she
pricked the finger, her mother had to leave off whatever she was doing and give first aid, the rest of the family had to scout around for
the thimble, which was a gold heirloom that belonged to her great-
grandmother, and which had rolled down a crack in the floor; and
the net result was that the schedule of the household was set back
anywhere from half an hour to half a day. My friend estimates that
for every stitch she tried to save in time, either she or those near and
dear to her lost an average of fifty stitches. Now, that could mount up
to quite a lot of embroidery in the course of a year: 18,250 stitches
a year, to be precise, or 18,300 in a leap year. A Bayeux tapestry
contains only 780,500 stitches. At least that would be my guess if I
were asked how many stitches a Bayeux contained.

What I didn't find out until too late was that each proverb has an
antidote proverb that cancels it. If a child knew the riposte proverb—which he never does, of course, since the adults hide the proverb books from the children—he could spring it, and thus leave his
parents without a leg to stand on. Parents have occupied this position for some time now, so we need not be concerned about their
comfort in the matter. When my mother proposed that I spend a
summer afternoon sprinkling Paris green on the potato plants, suggesting that Satan found work for idle hands to do, I could have told
her that all work and no play makes Jack a dull boy, but I was too innocent to be aware of such effective badinage at the time. The antidote for the one about never putting off until tomorrow is better late
than never, of course. Clothes make the man? Yes, but don't judge a
book by its cover. Absence makes the heart grow fonder. Yeah, and
familiarity breeds contempt. Honesty is the best policy, but Heaven
helps those who help themselves. Marry in haste, repent at leisure.
I cancel you that with nothing ventured, nothing gained. Bachelors,

male and female, willing and unwilling, are fond of quoting the one about marry in haste.

That's what I don't like about proverbs. They're two-faced. They mean whatever you want them to mean, on whatever grindstone you want to whet your ax. It's girls who are furious because they can't whistle who go around quoting, A whistling girl and a crowing hen always come to some bad end.

I was in my teens before I saw that one disproved. Martha disproved it. Many a girl who has never tooted a toot has come to a terrible end, but we who were Martha's schoolmates were too green to know that. Martha was a girl of great charm, who whistled. We liked her, and dreaded the day when we'd get to school to learn that she had been gored by a bull, or whisked off by a tornado, or been taken up by the constabulary for illicit whistling in the second degree. We thought it unfair that a girl, who in every other respect was a cinch to become leader of her scout troop, had to be rubbed out because of one failing, which seemed to us not a failing at all but a part of her charm.

Well, she fooled the maxim flingers. She remained uncowed by that proverb and practiced her whistling with such zeal she got to be a specialist in bird calls. She imitated only the very best quality songsters, like the Baltimore oriole, the yellow-throated vireo, and the Ossamaguntchie shreep, and it may be fairly assumed that these eminent birds were only too flattered to be imitated by a girl who had so courageously defied the calcified wisdom of the centuries. Martha married a man who could play seven musical instruments at once, including, if I recall correctly, the glockenspiel. She met him on the Chautauqua circuit, where she was making a good living doing her bird calls. I don't think you could call that a bad end for Martha. I mean, marrying a one-man orchestra. Well, it's at least debatable.

Long ago, when one of my mother's cronies would call on her and they would go to work in a nice, neighborly way on some absent sister, my mother would sometimes say, in a righteous tone, "Well, tell me who your company is and I'll tell you what you are."

Why? Why would my mother need to know who, for instance, my company was in order to know what I was? She knew me. I was her youngest son. She never had any trouble identifying me. When she wanted something from the store she would say, trippingly, with no faltering, "Frank, run down to Winship's and get me a package of cornstarch, two yeast cakes, and a pound of tub butter."

She did not say to me, "Little boy, kindly tell me who your company is."

ME: "Gladly, Mrs. Sullivan. My company consists chiefly of Willy Dunston, Florrie Esther Wall, Charlie Graves, Frank Graves, and Grace Lee."

MRS. SULLIVAN: "Why, now that I know your company, I know what you are. You're my son, Frank. Run down to Winship's, Frank, and get me a package of cornstarch, etc., etc."

(Little boys were always supposed to *run* errands, but they rarely did; they walked 'em.)

My mother and her friends had another proverb that puzzled me. They were fond of telling each other that fine words buttered no parsnips. Well, sure. Obviously. It seemed clear to my untutored mind that fine words had very little chance of buttering parsnips, not enough chance to make it worth while trying. Why butter a parsnip anyhow, even with butter? Beets, or asparagus, yes. But parsnips? A deplorable vegetable at best. No wonder proverbs bewilder children. There is less than meets the eye in so many of them.

The proof of this is that proverbs usually read just as well backward, or jumbled up. Fine words do not a parsnip make nor iron bars a summer. Butter ye parsnips while ye may, old time is still a-flying—ah, but we lapse into lyric poetry. It takes nine tailors to save a stitch in time. Now, that has just as authentic a ring as the original. Have you ever tried to coax nine tailors into repairing a suit in time to wear it to a party?

Perhaps we should have a general reconditioning, or reupholstering, of proverbs. It could be done without too much trouble, and economically. New materials would not be needed. The old materials that Shakespeare and his great contemporary, Anon, used are still as good as new, and can't be bettered. You can't get stuff like that today. A simple rearrangement of a batch of the more prominent proverbs might do everybody a lot of good.

Something on this order: A man is known by the Russian he scratches. A bird in the bush is worth two on Nellie's hat. An apple a day is the evil thereof. He that keeps the doctor away will live to fight another day. A penny saved is a pound foolish. Beauty is only the spice of life. You see, they sound just as sensible as the originals, and if delivered by an adult in a solemn, minatory voice, will convince a youngster of his own unworthiness as thoroughly as if they made sense. The youngster will not stop to analyze them or parse them. A parsed proverb blows nobody good.

A fool and his money rush in where angels fear to tread. That is just as true as the original version. A word to the wise is resented. Sleeping dogs make strange bedfellows. A woman's work is all play. Now, that one is much livelier than its original and, though not true, has the great merit of being almost sure to start a good, bang-up argument if quoted by a man to a woman. You can't have your cake. That's a streamlined version of an old maxim reshaped to fit current high prices. I got the idea from the memorable and shrewd improvement a contributor to F.P.A.'s "Conning Tower" once made upon a familiar saw. His version was: All work and no play makes jack. Much pithier than the original and, if telegraphed, gives you a three-word leeway in which to add some personal message like "Love to all" or "Grandmother just remarried."

Furthermore, I have just the man to take charge of mixing up our maxims. My man has a wonderful habit of making remarks that never seem to come out the way he planned. A friend asked if he had seen a certain play and if he had liked it. "Oh, don't miss it if you can," said Dave. And once he brought an argument to an abrupt and triumphant conclusion with what, to date, is my favorite sentence: "Well, I may be wrong but I'm not far from it."

An Innocent in Texas

I HAD HEARD so much about Texas that I was consumed with curiosity about our great sister republic to the south. Was it true
for instance that all Texans are seven feet tall except the football players at Texas Christian and Southern Methodist, who are
eight? Was it true that Rhode Island would fit 220 times into
Texas, as Texas friends had so often assured me? Was it true
that in the early years of the war there were so many Texans in
the Royal Canadian Air Force that Canadians were often temp-
ted to call it the Royal Canadian Air Force? Did Oveta Culp
Hobby . . .

I wanted to learn the answers. I wanted to see Texas in action.
There was only one way to do so. Throwing a few things into my bag
I took off for Houston. I travelled light—a spare ten-gallon hat, two
pairs of chaps, one for business and one for formal evening wear, a
lariat, a few other necessaries, and Rhode Island, which I brought
along because, in the interests of accuracy, I was eager to check on
that 220 story.

On a typical sparkling Texas morning I debarked at Houston. Two
glorious suns were shining, the regular one and the special Texas
sun. Above the hum of the city's traffic rose the pleasant susurrus
of Texas voices exchanging matutinal howdies in their melodious
Confederate drawl.

From the distance came the agreeable gurgle of gushers gushing

120

in the gusheries scattered about the city, with occasionally the triumphant yodel of an oil millionaire who had just discovered a new
gusher. Anon, the crack of rifle fire and the sight of a fleeing cattle
rustler with a posse at his heels told me plainer than words that Texas
could still dispense frontier justice.

"Yippee!" I cried, for I speak Texan fluently, and, drawing two or
three six-shooters from my belt, I fired a volley of twenty-one guns
in salute to Pecos Bill, John Nance Garner, General Santa Anna,
Stephen F. Austin, Maury Maverick and the Alamo.

I made Houston my first port of call because it is the metropolis
and chief city of the Texan republic, although I add instantly that
Dallas, San Antonio, Galveston, Waco, Wichita Falls, Fort Worth,
Austin, Abilene and El Paso are also the chief cities of Texas. Other
chief cities may have sprung up since I left. If so, I beg their pardon
for not mentioning them.

Houston has a population of 600,000 and, Houstonians informed
me, is growing at the rate of 10,000 inhabitants a day, 5000 of
them oil millionaires. Texas grows the largest and most luscious
grapefruit in the world and the richest millionaires. Jesse Jones of
Houston is the richest Jones in recorded history. At its present rate
of growth Houston will outstrip London and New York in a decade.
Perhaps sooner, since Texans are twice as big as Londoners or New
Yorkers.

My day in Houston was packed with excitement. No sooner was I
settled in my suite at one of the city's finer hotels than they struck oil
in the cellar and immediately started tearing down the twenty-eight-
story hotel to make way for the more profitable gusher. The hospi-
table Chamber of Commerce quickly found me agreeable quarters
in a twenty-nine-story hotel and after washing up I still had time
before lunch to measure Rhode Island into Houston. It goes seven
times.

I shall not soon forget that lunch. We had steak. Steak is the state
flower of Texas. Texas has the finest steaks and the best department
stores in the country. I had heard of the Gargantuan meals to which
the lusty Texans are accustomed, but after all I come from New
York, the home of the late Diamond Jim Brady, who thought nothing of consuming, at one sitting, twelve dozen oysters, eight quarts
of orange juice, four adult lobsters, two planked steaks and Lillian
Russell, so I set to work with a will and in no time at all was pridefully

chasing the last shred of tenderloin around my plate with a piece of bun.

"Yippee!" I remarked. "Here's one dam-yank that can tie on the old feedbag with any varmint in Houston."

Just then a waiter put a steak in front of me twice as big as the steak I had just eaten. The waiter was twice as big as a New York waiter.

"What's that thar, pardner?" says I.

"That thar's yore steak, pardner," says he.

"What was that thar I just et?" says I.

"That thar was jest yore hors d'oeuvre," says he.

"Yippee!" says I, but in a more chastened tone, you may be sure, and that was the last time I bragged of my appetite in Texas.

I tried to tell my hosts how overjoyed I was to be having my first glimpse of their great republic.

"Perhaps no other planet in the universe has contributed as many notable figures to history as Texas," I enthused. "Look at the roster—Martin Dies, Ma Ferguson, Sam Houston, Chester A. Nimitz, Ensign Gay, Abraham Lincoln, George Washington, Queen Victoria, Amon G. Carter, Napoleon Bonaparte, O. Henry, Charlemagne, John the Baptist, the Twelve Apostles . . ."

"Excuse me, pardner," interrupted a Texan, "only nine of the Twelve Apostles was from Texas."

After lunch my hosts asked me if there was anything in particular I wished to see, and I was able to answer them precisely.

"Before I leave Houston I want to see a new gusher come into being," I said.

"Easiest thing in the world. Step this way."

We went to a vacant lot down back of the post office, and the chairman of the Houston Gusher Commission took a folding divining rod from his pocket.

"What kind of oil would you all care to see, pardner?" he asked.

"Some of that black gold I've heard so much about, if you please," said I.

Thereupon the chairman mumbled a few charms, dangled the rod over a cactus plant nearby, and within seconds there was a grumble. There followed a restless groaning and heaving as of oil struggling to reach the surface, the cactus plant hurried off in a kind of panic, and a second later on that very spot a fine geyser of high-octane black gold shot ninety-two feet into the air before us.

"Golly!" I exclaimed, in awesome admiration. "Congratulations. I'll wager this gusher will bring you fellows a pretty penny in royalties."

"Why, she's yours," cried the chairman, jovially.

"Oh, no. Really, I couldn't think . . ."

"Nonsense. It's your luncheon favor. Compliments of the Chamber of Commerce of Houston. We always give gushers to visitors. Why don't you christen her?"

"I christen thee the Pappy O'Daniel," I said to the oil well, and instantly it gulped, gasped and retreated into the bowels of the earth.

"Better try another name," the chairman suggested.

"I christen thee the Davy Crockett," I amended, and this time the gusher gushed joyfully again. I can only add that that gusher has to date brought me $4,390,000 in royalties. As far as I am concerned the accounts of the legendary hospitality of Houston are definitely not exaggerated.

Nor are the accounts of the legendary hospitality of Dallas exaggerated. Dallas, named for Stella Dallas, is 187 light years distant from Houston and is the finest city in Texas. By a stroke of good fortune I visited Dallas just at a time when the traditional rivalry between itself and Fort Worth, the finest city in Texas, had reached one of its periodical boiling points. It seems that the night before I got there a band of marauders from Fort Worth had made a surprise attack on the famous Nieman-Marcus department store in Dallas and with shouts of "Yippee!" and "Southern Methodist is no good, chop 'em up for kindling wood!" had carried off the entire contents of the notion counter, along with several hundred pounds of pecan pralines. Feeling was running high in Dallas and there was talk of reprisals on the Fort Worth Cowboy Lament Works, the great sprawling industrial plant where 20,000 musicians work in three shifts composing the dirges which have made the name of Texas so—what shall I say?—throughout the world.

The rivalry between the various cities of Texas is an interesting phenomenon and, I was told, is the main reason why the founders of the republic felt it wise to place each city at least 800 miles from its nearest neighbor. In telling a Dallasian his community is not as matchless a civic gem as Fort Worth you run an even greater risk than if you told an Irishman from Connemara that County Mayo is the flawless emerald in Erin's diadem.

The Easterner, or tenderfoot, will not comprehend this keen, internecine rivalry. A resident of, let us say, Rochester has no fear of not being made welcome when he visits New York City (one of the larger cities in the state). True, his wallet may be extracted from his pants before he has got three blocks from the Grand Central Terminal, but it is done quietly and with a minimum of discomfort to him. He will be overcharged at hotels and restaurants and will pay one of the better kings' ransoms for theatre tickets and on his way home he may be mugged by an acquisitive thug, but it is all in a spirit of detachment, like a surgeon removing a gall bladder. There is absolutely no bias against him simply because he comes from Rochester. In fact, the driver of the taxi which clips him as he crosses Fifth Avenue may himself be a Rochester boy. Truly it is a small world in New York.

Not soon shall I forget my first sight of Fort Worth. I neared the city on foot from the east, meaning east of Fort Worth, at about sunset. My two slaves, Caesar and Pompey, whom I had picked up for a song in one of the large Houston department stores, followed me at a respectful distance, carrying Rhode Island. On the western horizon, enclosing the city in a shimmering, iridescent halo, was a sight of such beauty as to take away my breath—and I had little of it to spare after the day's hike. Reds, golds, crimsons, purples, pinks, mauves, oranges, bananas, a thousand delicate hues intermingled in what cannot but be described as a veritable riot of color. Never, not even over the Hackensack meadows, had I seen so gorgeous a sunset, and for that reason if for none other my disappointment was the keener when I learned that it was not a sunset at all but the great Fort Worth Cowboy Shirt Plant, where they make all those beautiful, vivid shirts that cowboys wear to frighten steers into submission. What I mistook for a sunset was the day's output of the shirt mills, hung out to air. I shall never again see a sunset that will not seem tame.

One of the most agreeable episodes of my trip to Texas was the day I spent on the Regal Ranch, the largest cattle, or any kind of, ranch in the world. Rhode Island fitted into it sixty-seven times. It is so large that although there are 949 billion trillions of blades of grass

on it, each blade is three feet from its nearest neighbor. (I am in-
debted to Professor Harlow Shapley of the Harvard Department of
Astronomy for the use of these figures.) The cattle have to be flown
in jet planes from one pasturage to another. If they tried to walk they
would either die of fatigue or become so tough and muscle-bound
that they would be useless for anything except one of those $8 table
d'hôte dinners at a swank New York hotel. No matter how large you
think the Regal Ranch is, it is twice as large as that. In fact the cowboys from the northern part of the ranch can scarcely understand
the dialect spoken by their colleagues from its southern shires.

Last year the Regal exported 5,476,397 head of cattle to Kansas
City and 2,397,739 head of cowboy to the Hollywood mart. Of the
latter, 726,387 were pure Roy Rogers, 327,835 were Gene Autrys
and 14,397 were genuine, antique Gary Coopers. The foreman of
one of the counties in the ranch told me they are experimenting on
an improved breed of cowboy, who will combine the best features of
all cowboys since William S. Hart and will, as one improved feature,
have fingernails four times as durable as the present ones, and therefore be better equipped for successful plunking of guitars. Many an
otherwise magnificent specimen of cowboy, the foreman told me,
has had to be shot because of brittle fingernail, an occupational
defect which renders a cowhand useless as a guitar strummer and
hence useless. The fingernail snaps off in the middle of "Home on
the Range," and lasting shame is the lot of the unfortunate cowboy,
through no fault of his own.

With his plunking fingernail thus bolstered, the last defect will
be removed from the Texas cowboy, and he will be the most perfect
specimen of fine upstanding manhood the world has known. He is
eight feet tall, of course. No cowhand under that height can hope to
win his lariat. He is not only a paragon of manly beauty but he has a
pure mind and worships the ground that women walk on. Woman-
kind, whom he traditionally and respectfully addresses as "Ma'am,"
takes second place in his affections only to the little dogies whose
virtues he has lyricised to the envy of all the rest of the animal king-
dom, no species of which has found so eloquent a minstrel to sing
its praises. The Texas cowhand is generous to a fault and, unless you
are wary, he will give you the shirt off his back. Quick to resent an
affront he nevertheless has a heart of gold, and no widow or orphan
ever appealed to him for succor in vain.

I shall not name, for I would not dignify him by doing so, a certain viper whom I encountered at a luncheon given for me by the Chamber of Commerce of one of the larger cattle ranches. Chatting casually with this person, who had been introduced to me as a Texan, I said, "You've got a mighty fine state down here, pardner."

"Oh, it's all right," he said, in a tone of diffidence which I did not quite like.

"It's the biggest state in the Union," I said, bridling slightly.

"Size isn't everything," he remarked.

I was now pretty nettled, for in my stay I had come to look upon Texas with great affection.

"Texas has won every war for the United States," I challenged.

"Pooh!" This from a Texan!

"You pooh Texas!" I cried, astounded.

"Yes, and I re-pooh it," said he.

"You deny Texas won the World wars in addition to the Spanish-American, Civil and Revolutionary wars?"

"I do. Where do you come from?"

"Round Lake, New York."

"I thought so. You foreigners who become enamored of Texas brag worse than our own Chamber of Commerce. Texas is just another state."

I know I acted hastily. I should have turned him over to the Chamber of Commerce. But I couldn't help it. I shot him. No jury convicted me.

A week had passed and my visit to the Lonesome Star State was coming to a close. I do not pretend to have seen all of Texas in my week there. It would take at least another week to do that. But I had completed my research with Rhode Island. It really does go 220 times into Texas. In fact, I had Deaf Smith County left over.

Feel My Muscle

I HAVE BEEN contemplating the cover of one of those muscle magazines devoted to body culture. The cover is a photograph of a bulgy young Samson clad in a pair of bathing trunks. He stands on a boulder at the seashore in an attitude of thought. My guess is that the thought is about himself and what a perfect physical specimen he is. At his feet the surf can be seen, presumably murmuring in admiration, and in the background there is a long steel pier, which he probably plans to lift as soon as he finishes thinking.

The young man has a good face, though not one to cause the beholder to cry, "Ah, *there's* a coming atomic physicist!" He has got his chest stuck out as far as it will go, and it goes an alarming distance. Starting just below his Adam's apple, it juts out so horizontally for about a foot that you could serve tea on it and hardly spill a drop. All his other muscles are in proportion, or out of proportion, depending on your point of view. My point of view is as follows:

I wish I could get in touch with that deluded youth and persuade him to quit chinning himself before it is too late. He is not the perfect specimen he thinks he is. Providence never designed any youth to be so muscle-bound. I can make these comments without suspicion of sour grapes. I have reached an age when I look just as good standing on my head as I do right side up; but at least my bay window is where Nature intended bay windows to be, not up under my chin.

The truth is, I fear, that there is a love affair between this young man and himself. It is clear from the way he is posing. He is strutting while standing still.

If he were the only youth in the country with a top-heavy chest and biceps built for two, artificially induced by gymnasium gadgets as opposed to normal manual labor, one could shed a compassionate tear for his plight and pass on to worry about larger problems. But from what I hear and read, a great many young men all over the country are devoting a great deal of time and energy to making themselves look as much as possible like Popeye after he has eaten the spinach. Don't they ever invite their *souls?* The mind as well as the body has sinews, of a kind, which ought to be developed. In days when I thought nothing of touching the floor without bending my knees, there was a sign in the gymnasium at Cornell University that read, *"Mens sana in corpore sano."* We students of the Arts College translated this motto for the vets, engineers, chemists, agronomists, and other students of the less couth colleges, as "A sound mind in a sound body."

I could give that budding Popeye on the cover some friendly advice on the perils of exercise, because—confession is good for the soul—I am a reformed gymnast myself. I have a dumbbell in my closet alongside the skeletons. One winter I became depressed by the fact that I was becoming pear shaped, and with the touching illusion that a pudgy chap of thirty-five can keep from becoming pear shaped, I enrolled in a private gym patronized by champion golfers, boxers, and other non-pear-shaped persons. I went there every afternoon and tossed the medicine ball with a strapping instructor, whom, I am rather pleased to say, I think I bored as much as he bored me. As I couldn't, or wouldn't, wear my spectacles in the gym and couldn't see without them, I never caught the medicine ball. It always caught me, and right where I was most pear shaped, too. I am sure that young Hercules planned it that way.

When we weren't tossing the medicine ball, he had me doing incredible tricks, like standing on my neck and waving my legs in the air. Today I might get paid for doing that in Macy's window; but in those days I not only calisthenicked for nothing but paid the gym proprietor to let me do so. I stood abjectly on my neck for two months, too proud to give up, or afraid to uncrick my neck, and then, fortunately, got lobar pneumonia, which served as an alibi for my quitting that gym. I feel sure my subconscious arranged that pneumonia to give me the alibi. Realizing that I was too pear shaped to become an athlete, I gave up, and haven't exercised since.

If that young weight lifter on the cover thinks he is working toward the Greek ideal of physical perfection, he is on the wrong track, bless his poor, over-strained heart. The Greeks were no fools. They never allowed their torsos to grow knotted and gnarled. Their ideal was symmetry. Their muscles never bulged. They rippled. The Greeks did not cultivate barrel chests and wasp waists. Judging from his statues, Apollo was even a bit thick at the waist, yet he got along fine on Mount Olympus and worked his way up to be one of the more influential of the gods. A place for every muscle and every muscle in its place was the motto of the Greeks, and they never stood for any nonsense from bumptious biceps seeking special notice.

I must also warn young Samson that if he thinks he is enhancing his appeal to the opposite sex by over-developing his chest to such an excess, he is taking a chance there, too. While not averse to physical charm in the male, girls today view it with a more practical eye than in the days when Elinor Glyn wowed the rest of her sex with "Three Weeks." Most girls are also good at arithmetic today, and they realize that if they marry an Adonis who is already in love with himself, he will be able to spare them only half as much love as they would get from a partner indifferent to his own charms but rapturously entranced by those of his wife.

There is another risk hovering over young Samson. He may exercise until the law of diminishing returns sets in, when he will not be able to exercise at all. Most mothers have come in contact with this law in a mild form, having had experience with sons who, though intrepid and tireless fullbacks on the high-school eleven, or distinguished forwards on the basketball team, pale visibly if requested to fetch a scuttle of coal.

Paradoxically, the more athletic athletes become the less they seem able to cope with that drab form of athletics known as chores, or making yourself handy around the home. The causes? It may be that after an apprentice Ajax has put in four hours at the gym lifting heavy weights, he has no strength left for chopping kindling wood. It may be that he feels mowing a lawn is a frivolous task for a fellow with a chest measure of sixty-seven expanded and biceps that really amount to triceps. Like asking a giant crane to hoist a bobby pin.

There is one rule to follow. When your biceps have developed to a point where it makes your friends wince to look at them, quit exercising until they subside to normal. Just don't bulge.

Boxers don't bulge. Anyone with a television set can see that. Intercollegiate champion swimmers do not bulge and, if Coach can spare them, are often of invaluable assistance to their mothers in beating rugs or bringing the porch furniture up from the cellar in April. Broad jumpers and mile runners do not consider it essential that their chests be three times the dimensions of their waists, any more than a Parisienne feels she must adopt the lip fashions prevalent among the more chic Ubangi women. Baseball players do not bulge, and the more aged among them, those approaching thirty, frequently flaunt the suspicions of a bay window, and are thought none the less of for it.

In conclusion I should like to state that many of the above warnings apply to drum majorettes as well as to young Samsons. Drum majorettes have become increasingly numerous since the American Legion started having parades about 1920, and they are, in a way, the opposite number to the weight lifters. They are bulging. It comes from all that strutting, and gyrating, and r'arin' back, and pretzeling of the torso they are called on to go through in the course of their parade duties. They are in grave danger of becoming hopelessly convex where they should be concave, and concave where they should be convex.

First Robin — and the First New Calluses

THE FIRST ROBIN, the sugar storm, the first crocus. Yes, to be sure they are signs of spring; or harbingers, to use the correct technical term. We nature lovers must be precise about the terms we use. I once heard of a worthy woman who was publicly stripped of her trowel and dibble and drummed out of her garden club for referring to a tang of spring when she meant a breath of spring. Tang is, of course, what there is of autumn in the air. The lady's colleagues felt, regretfully, that one who did not know this could not be safely entrusted with the education of a nasturtium.

There are many harbingers of spring, so many that it is a wonder we are able to establish definitely when The Vernal is really here. There is, for instance, the day when little girls and boys come strolling home from school carrying their coats instead of wearing them. Each year I suspect this may mark the beginning of spring, but the next day it snows and all the children who took off their coats are home with colds.

The harbingers are not all external. There is an inner urge that signals the approach of spring to a householder as surely as the stirring of the sap must signal it to the maple. When the sun rolls north and the bear yawns, the householder feels within him the immortal urge to rake, the craving to Tidy Up and get rid of the debris of winter. The snow shovel is stacked in its summer niche in the cellar, provided it has been returned by the small neighbor who borrowed it after the blizzard in January so that he might pick up a couple of bucks shovelling sidewalks for widows. The rake is dusted off. The calluses peculiar to the snow shovel must now adjust themselves to the rake. There is a difference between the two—they tell me.

One day the young man's fancy lightly turns to thoughts of love and/or whether it would be wiser to enlist now or finish his college year, but on that day the young man's father's fancy is not turning to thoughts of love. The young man's father's fancy has been all through love years ago, else the young man would not be here. What the old man's fancy is turning to is getting down those storm windows and dismantling the snow guards which have protected the shrubbery along the side of the house from avalanches and icicles.

The fastenings of the snow guards have rusted, the dinguses stick, and if the householder is one of those misfits of the mechanical age whose fingers are all thumbs, he is up against it unless he has friendly neighbors with the knack of dismantling snow guards successfully. Your bethumbed chronicler is happy in the possession of such neighbors.

Spring advances with small steps forward and back, like a minuet or, as it sometimes seems, like a combination of a minuet and a rumba. At each step forward a little more snow disappears. Is there anything that looks more melancholy than a dying snowbank? I hope no one will bother to answer that question in the illusion that the reward is $64. It is one of the sure external signs of spring when snowbanks that once dazzled the eye in the December sun or shone blue-white in the January twilight dwindle to tawdry, granulated piles, embroidered with winter's mourning, those lacy black traceries that represent four months' accumulation of grime from the neighborhood furnaces.

A moribund snowbank protected by a northern exposure can display a surprising tenacity of life. I came upon one such on a warm day about the first of May last year while walking through Yaddo, a sanctuary in my town where birds and creative artists can find refuge from the hunter. On this spring day the birds were singing, the buds were budding and little fluffy clouds were nipping across the empyrean like chicks after a bug. Yet under the cool protection of the northwest corner of the great mansion there was a preposterous anachronism of a snowbank, discouraged but stubborn. I hardly recognized the stuff, so quickly does merciful nature draw a veil of forgetfulness over memories of an upstate winter.

A year ago, in a spirit of scientific inquiry, I made notes each day on the progress of spring. I suppose the notes are valid this spring, one spring being much like another unless we have been grossly deceived by our poets. My note for March 31, reads, "As snow melts messy debris of winter discloses itself." Very penetrating observation, and no gainsaying it!

As the snowbanks die they yield the flotsam of the winter: a soggy mitten lost by a tot in a January romp on the way home from school; an old tin can long since bereft of the tomato juice or peas of which it was once the repository; an abandoned Christmas card; a charred section of a bill from Altman's which a breeze snatched from the incinerator; some bottle caps; a bone buried by a pup with a foolish trust in the permanency of snow; a faded valentine, and perhaps even that missing New Year's celebrant who wandered out of the party into the night at 3 o'clock New Year's morning and has not been seen since.

There comes the inevitable day when the householder must brace himself to face the annual ordeal. His lawn is finally clear of snow and he must look at it. It was so lush and verdant last summer, under his tender manicuring, and look at it now! A scrawny, half-starved, brown waste, picked out with dreadful leprous patches marking the spots where, though with the best of intentions, he overdid the doses of bone meal last November. Will it ever again look like a respectable lawn? It will.

One of my more sententious notes reads, "Pungent odor of spring, decayed leaves, etc." How true, as anyone knows who has smelled the aroma of damp leaves in April or caught the redolence of an etc. returning to life under the warmth of the sun. The Vernal does indeed have its special bouquet suggestive of the quickening earth, and quite unlike the dry, dusty, smoky smell—pardon, tang—of autumn.

The peculiar glitter in the eyes of the husbandman as he surveys his garden of a Sunday morning in April shows that he thinks it is about time he spaded. Soon the aroma of warm, new-turned earth will be added to the spring smells and the neighbors will exchange pertinent remarks like, "A warm rain would start things growing," or, "What we really need is a few days' sun."

Pretty soon the lawn begins to take heart and, lo! one day there is the first dandelion. Next day you may get one of those falls of wet, clinging snow in oversized, jumbo flakes which are called sugar storms because they are supposed to start the sap rising in the maples. In my neck of the woods we sometimes get so many sugar storms you would think the sap would be popping out of the topmost twigs in the maples. A few years ago, on May 10, a sugar blizzard hustled down upon Saratoga County from the Hudson's Bay region, left nine inches of snow, broke down tree limbs and power lines, flattened budding shrubbery and cut off the light and heat for a day or so. A final slap from winter, just as a reminder, in case anyone had the idea it was permanently vanquished.

The days come when the thermometer hits 70, the sap rises in the housekeeper and she gets the urge to clean house, first manifestation of which is a directive to her brother to haul up The Stuff from the cellar. The Stuff comprises stuff like garden tables and chairs, garden hose, porch furniture, grass mats, sprinklers, lawn mower, the bird bath and other estival paraphernalia. Then comes spring painting. This year I plan a vice versa approach to painting the porch. I will give myself two thorough coats of paint and hope that enough will stick to the verandas to make them presentable.

The yellow branches of the willow tree become outlined in the palest green. Two robins start a nest and a feud with the bluejays, simultaneously. The sober grey lacing of the elm branches shows green, too, and gets greener each day, and soon the bed of scarlet Emperor tulips looks as colorful as a conclave of cardinals. Harbingers have appeared in about the following order: crocus, forsythia, narcissus, daffodil, grape hyacinth, hyacinth, violets, forget-me-nots, tulips, dogwood, lilacs, lilies of the valley, the spirea bushes and the blossoms on the flowering crab and the old choke-cherry tree. I do not guarantee the accuracy of this procession. My status as a botanist and gardener is strictly amateur.

Spring marches north slowly but surely. The traveler notes that New York City gets it a good two weeks ahead of Saratoga Springs, 190 miles to the north. Even Albany, thirty-five miles south of the famed spa, is springier by two or three days, and is usually free of snow when the uplands of Saratoga County are still coated with it.

When can it be said spring is actually here? Maybe it is when the spruces start putting out those bright green paws that make the rest of the tree seem faded. Maybe it is when you look at the recently mottled lawn and find to your pleased surprise that it needs a haircut. Maybe spring is here on the day you hear and see that welcome little chap, the oriole, hopping about the upper branches of the elms, carolling his endorsement of the tender bugs on which he is dining. Maybe it is spring when the spirea hedge bursts into dazzling white bloom and, stirred by the western breeze, tosses like a hundred-foot snowbank in motion. Maybe it is spring when the seeds from the elms leave the parent and go a-wooing on the wings of the breeze. Maybe it is spring when journalists feel the urge to write sentences like the foregoing.

Some Notes I Have Met

I LIKE TO listen to music although I know nothing about it. At least, not much. I know that Mozart, Haydn and Beethoven are dead, and that certain modern composers ought to be. Mozart died at an early age from a surfeit of starvation, the result of being patronized by too many archdukes. Haydn was called Papa Haydn for what were probably sound reasons. Beethoven got slapped around so much in his boyhood by a cranky father that he became deaf in later life. This gives me something in common with Beethoven, as I was also deafened one night in Carnegie Hall, many years ago, at the first, and maybe the last, performance of the George Antheil symphony for eight Klaxons, a brace of cowbells, a buzz saw, a washboiler, a Model-T fender, and the contents of Fibber McGee's hall closet. I may have left out a few of the instruments Mr. Antheil employed but the brunt of the theme was borne by those I mention. I survived that memorable event in the history of music, and so did Mr. Antheil, who successfully eluded his pursuers and lived to repent.

Let me see if I can impart any other musical lore. Well, I know that in every symphony worth its salt there is a majestic movement representing the March of Fate. You can tell the March of Fate by watching the kettledrum player. If he shows signs of working up a sweat, you know you're well into the March of Fate. Fate marches around a good deal in "Beethoven's Fifth." Fate keeps popping in and out of the "Fifth" like the Marx Brothers in the bedroom scene, when Harpo is chasing the blonde. You will also find Fate frequently on the march in Brahms and Sibelius, like a Gloomy Old Gentleman walking up and down the keyboard saying, "So you think you feel well, eh? Just wait until you try to move your head." Fate is expressed chiefly by the tympani in the orchestra and that is why tympanists, or kettledrummers, who work in orchestras where Brahms, Beethoven and Sibelius are played a great deal are poor insurance risks. They wear out early.

I know also that Beethoven won the late war by means of the Morse code, which was a mighty good trick when you consider that neither Samuel F. B. Morse nor his code had been invented when Beethoven wrote that dot-dot-dot-dash "V" motif for the opening of the "Fifth."

Other tidbits about music come to mind. For instance, one appertaining to that commonly entertained myth that musicians have long, delicate, slender fingers. It is not true. With such a set of fingers a musician would not get to first base, which would be about the middle of the first half of the first movement of a Vivaldi concerto. I know what I'm talking about here because I did research on this point by scrutinizing sixteen of the most distinguished fingers that this country affords. They were on two fellows named Iturbi and Heifetz.

I had a good look at Iturbi's fingers, at close range, at a champagne supper given for the maestro in Saratoga one October night ten years ago. He was appearing there with his Rochester Philharmonic, and his sister Amparo, a merry and brilliant girl, was soloist. Mac Kriendler of the Club Twenty-One in New York was in Saratoga at the time taking the cure, and to pass the time away he grew one of the most beautiful sets of pink whiskers I have ever seen. Pardon me, I withdraw that hedging qualification. They *were* the most beautiful pink whiskers I ever saw. I asked Mr. Kriendler to give me those whiskers when he left, but he failed to oblige. I wanted to weave them into a tapestry I was making as part of my occupational therapy. Where were we? Ah, yes. Well, Mac threw a party for José and Amparo, and it was a very fine party, and that was the night I had a close look at José Iturbi's fingers. They are not long and delicate. They are muscular and strong and stout, and fit for the work they have to do. The same is true of Jascha Heifetz's fingers, of which I also had a close-up on several occasions.

Why not? Why shouldn't the hands of a virtuoso be supple and strong? How could he be a virtuoso if they were otherwise? Any set of muscles constantly in use is bound to be well-developed. The build of nine out of ten Wagnerian sopranos bears out this theory. You never see any chicken-breasted sopranos.

Other interesting facts about music occur: Chopin was delicate of health and fell in love with George Sand, although she wore slacks and smoked cigars. Today Chopin would be rushed to a psycho-analyst for doing a thing like that. Toscanini is allergic to photographers. Verdi slept in the raw. So did Emma Calvé. It is rumored that Paganini once played a concerto wearing fur mittens. Jenny Lind slept in a crinoline and people came from far and near to witness the awesome spectacle. All composers of modern music sleep in the raw. Neighbors of composers of modern music do not sleep.

A sobering thought: a century from now what we know as modern music will be considered old-fashioned. This thought almost makes one reconciled to the possibility that there may not be any twenty-first century.

What becomes of those poor unfortunates who applaud a number at a concert before it is finished? I suppose they are never again received in correct musical circles, but I never read that one of them jumped off a high tower or flung himself into the river in despair over his humiliation.

I am not sure it is fair to outlaw these poor chumps just because they strive to please. Whenever I observe one of them committing this unpardonable sin at a concert I murmur, "There but for the grace of God go I." Because I had the foresight early in my musical career to go to concerts with a lady who knew when a piece was ended, and couldn't be fooled, and never cheered prematurely. She kept an eye on me, and when a phantom lull occurred in a piece and she saw me mistaking it for the end, she would seize my hands, and say, "Not yet." I would have been drummed out of Carnegie Hall in disgrace many years ago had it not been for Mrs. Campbell.

You have to watch your step. There are certain composers who are not above tricking the listener if they can. They back their symphony into a corner and start giving it the works. They get the bull fiddles and all the rest of the strings sawing away for dear life. They egg on the glockenspiel, the kettledrums, and the snare drums and they get the organist to pull out all stops, if he is in the outfield that game. Then they roar away with a great crash, boom, and clatter which can best be described as Wagnerian, until finally they come to a full stop. Can the innocent music lover, unacquainted with the pitfalls a concert hall may hold, be blamed if he assumes that this silence is the calm after the storm? The payoff. The Triumph of Destiny over Fate, or the entrance of the gods into Valhalla, or some musical apogee like that. In short, the end. Can he be blamed for bursting into wild applause?

He cannot, but he is. When the suckers in the concert hall have been trapped into such applause, and in some cases have even shouted "Bravo!" and "Bis!", the conductor lifts his baton and off goes the whole orchestra again, all stops open, no holds barred, pandemonium supreme, for another five minutes. Destiny, theretofore assumed to have triumphed over Fate, suffers a Bastogne, and Victory is delayed. And a lot of poor dubs never dare clap at a concert again, for fear of doing it at the wrong time.

This sort of fake ending is a shabby trick to play on the customers, and would not be tolerated in a baseball park or a football stadium. The victim ought to have a sporting chance at reprisal on composers and conductors who pull it.

I will conclude these random reminiscences with a true and charming story about that moody genius, Rachmaninoff. He visited my home town one winter night some years ago to give a concert at the local college. He put up at the local inn and an hour before concert time he came down to the parlor, seated himself at the hotel piano, which had not felt the attentions of a tuner in some time, struck a chord or two, winced perceptibly, and then began limbering up with a few scales.

The desk clerk on duty at the time, who told me this story, is an agreeable boy and not a fool, but he certainly could rush in. Having nothing to do at the moment he strolled into the parlor, greeted Rachmaninoff, and then this foolhardy worm asked Rachmaninoff to play something for him.

Rachmaninoff took it in his stride.

"Vot shall I play for you?" he asked.

"Do you know 'Tiger Rag'?" asked my friend George.

"No," said the maestro. "How does it go?"

Fifteen minutes later, when Rachmaninoff's manager came downstairs looking for him, he found the great pianist and the hotel clerk seated on the piano stool. The clerk was picking out what little he could of "Tiger Rag" to give the maestro an idea of how it went. The sad, Slavic Rachmaninoff was giving the utmost attention to his tutor, and doing the best he could to learn "Tiger Rag."

"Gee, he was a nice guy for a big shot," said George, as he told me the story.

The Cliché Expert Testifies
on the Tabloids

Q: MR. ARBUTHNOT, you are, I believe, an expert on the use of the cliché as applied by the tabloids to the recounting of news about love, murder, and other events of violence?

A: I am an alleged expert in that field.

Q: Why "alleged"?

A: Crime reporters *always* say "alleged."

Q: I see. Well, suppose we start with love. How is love doing in the tabs these days?

A: Oh, love is in a fine molten state, as usual.

Q: How do you know?

A: Because love life of wealthy socialite and blond eyeful is constantly being bared in court. Hollywood stars continue to scout rumors of rift. Broadway playboy seeks blood test in paternity suit, and vice is rife among teen-agers, says Supreme Court Judge. Father of ten continues to be jailed for annoying women, and morals of minors keep right on being impaired.

Q: Who would you say are the chief practitioners of love in the tabloids?

A: Well, the parties I just mentioned—except, of course, the Supreme Court Judge—also attractive blondes, petite blondes, striking blondes, dashing brunettes, statuesque beauties, hot mamas, erring mates, love prisoners, love slaves, pretty ex-models, honey-tressed hat-check girls, heirs to $50,000,000 fortunes, members of the Long Island hunting set, sex fiends, scions of old New York families, much-married film stars, and eighty-year-old women determined to wed hired hands fifty years their junior.

Q: Please sketch briefly the course of true love in the tabs.

A: Well, wealthy socialite meets blond eyeful, falls for her, showers her with attentions, then installs her in a swank penthouse apartment.

Q: Swank penthouse apartment is customarily referred to as love nest, is it not?

A: The phrase "love nest" has been a bit passé ever since the *Daily Graphic* collapsed, but you will find it used occasionally by the more nostalgic headline writers.

Q: After wealthy socialite installs blond eyeful in swank penthouse apartment, they become what?

A: They become intimate, or friendly. Their names are linked.

Q: And after that?

A: Eventually, love cools.

Q: You mean . . .

A: Romance sours. Romance of wealthy Park Avenue playboy and blond eyeful is shattered.

Q: Why?

A: Wealthy playboy falls for hat-check girl or he finds there are other men in blond eyeful's life.

Q: If the former is the case, what does blond eyeful do?

A: She takes his letters to court.

Q: The letters are known as what?

A: They are known as sizzling love missives.

Q: And when blond eyeful's lawyer is reading sizzling love missives in court, what does the judge do?

A: He orders the courtroom cleared.

Q: Mr. Arbuthnot, if wealthy playboy is married and becomes intimate or friendly with attractive blonde or dashing brunette, what does that make him in the eyes of the tabloids?

A: That makes him erring mate. By the way, people do not marry in the tabs. They wed. They have to, of course, so that later they can scout rumors of a rift.

Q: I see. What does wife of erring mate do?

A: She charges blond eyeful with stealing mate.

Q: That makes blond eyeful what?

A: That makes her a love pirate or love thief.

Q: And what kind of wife is wife of erring mate?

A: Injured wife.

Q: What course does injured wife adopt in dealing with erring mate?

A: She begs him to come back.

Q: And if he won't?

A: She seeks a divorce.

Q: Where?

A: At the divorce mill.

Q: Where is that?

A: In Reno. That, of course, makes erring mate and injured wife an estranged pair. Marriage is on rocks.

Q: By the way, Mr. Arbuthnot, is erring mate always a man?

A: Heck, no! Many erring mates are of the gentler sex.

Q: Such a mate has what?

A: She has male admirers, hubby charges, and he seeks custody of children, alleging her unfit mother.

Q: In a case like that, if male admirer rats on unfit mother and testifies for hubby, what does that make him?

A: That makes him kiss-and-tell lover.

Q: In addition to swank-penthouse form of love, what other varieties do the tabloids recognize?

A: Well, they are rather partial to a cruder form of the grand passion.

Q: Tell us about it, please.

A: It is the form in which a less urbane type of male, when obsessed by love, annoys women.

Q: What do you mean, "annoys"?

A: That's a journalistic euphemism for "molest."

Q: And what is "molest"?

A: That's another euphemism, for "accost," which is a euphemism for "attack," which is a euphemism for—ah, but I do not wish to encroach upon the Kinsey Report. You look it up there.

Q: Now, Mr. Arbuthnot, let us make the slight transition from love to murder. How many kinds of homicide do the tabloids recognize?

A: There are thirteen major categories: love slayings, hitchhike murders, axe murders, cold-blooded slayings, defense killings, poison mysteries, mercy killings, revenge killings, knife slayings, hammer murders, trunk murders, gangland killings, and teen-age murders. In none of these can the slayer remember firing the fatal shot, or its equivalent.

Q: Who commit most of the murders in the tabloids?

A: It is generally conceded that a near-monopoly in this field is held by discharged farm laborers, ex-convicts, disgruntled handymen, high-school honor students, exotic night-club dancers, hubbies, ex-hubbies, wives, ex-wives, love-crazed suitors, underworld figures, or trigger men, maniacs lusting for blood, discarded mistresses, casual acquaintances, and men seen lurking in the vicinity the day of the crime. But society is the real culprit.

Q: I see. Of what complexion is your run-of-the-mill murderer?

A: Of swarthy complexion, if male, and especially if he has been seen lurking. If the killer is a lady, the copy desk would prefer that she be a blonde—exotic, if possible.

Q: How is the body discovered?

A: In a pool of blood.

Q: By whom?

A: Children at play, or casual passersby. They stumble on it.

Q: And where is it discovered?

A: In a dense thicket, stolen auto, lonely ravine, thickly wooded area, abandoned shack, tourist cabin, furnished room, the East River, love hideaway, lonely spot, or a clump of underbrush only a few yards from a busy highway. And do you know what the police suspect?

Q: No.

A: Well, you can bet your boots it isn't *fair* play. Ask me what is known to the police.

Q: Consider it asked.

A: The identity of the slayer.

Q: Mr. Arbuthnot, if the body is found in a furnished room, what does the room show?

A: Marks of a struggle, or evidences of same.

Q: If in an auto, in what position?

A: Slumped.

Q: In revenge killings, what statement does the killer make to the police?

A: He says, "Hate welled up within me. Next thing I knew, she was lying there on the floor." Or she says it, and he was lying there on the floor.

Q: How do the police tell a revenge killing?

A: By the purse. If contents of purse are intact, it was revenge. If purse is rifled and valuable diamond ring victim was known to be wearing is missing, robbery was the motive.

Q: What causes teen-age killings?

A: Postwar letdown, honor students falling into clutches of Fagins, vice rampant at high-school proms, cheap movies, radio crime serials, and reefers.

Q: What precedes murders in which victim is dumped from auto, or found slumped, or dragged to above-mentioned clump?

A: An all-night tour of the roadhouses or honky-tonks. Suspect admits he and slain woman had been drinking heavily and had had altercation.

Q: Prior to a murder, what often exists between the parties to same?

A: Bad blood.

Q: Possibly the result of a quarrel over what?

A: Women or baseball.

Q: Not money?

A: Money comes third.

Q: Now, then, Mr. Arbuthnot, when police arrest a suspect—

A: Pardon me. Police never arrest in the tabloids. Cops nab. Yet you never call a cop. You summon the police. Tabloid usage is often as puzzling to grasp as French irregular verbs.

Q: Well, when cops nab suspect, how do they hold him?

A: Incommunicado.

Q: Why?

A: They want to question him, or grill him. That is, wring a confession from him.

Q: Do cops ever get a confession by any other method than by wringing?

A: Oh, no. The tabloids would spurn any cop who failed to wring.

Q: Why do the cops get, or wring, the confession?

A: Well, naturally, if they don't, the alleged slayer could not repudiate the confession at his trial, alleging police brutality.

Q: What else do the cops do to the slayer?

A: They make him reënact the slaying at the scene of the crime.

Q: Who are present at these dramas?

A: Detectives, photographers, Police Commissioner, reporters, and morbid curiosity seekers.

Q: Mr. Arbuthnot, when hardened characters bump each other off, what is that known as?

A: That's a gangland killing.

Q: How do gangsters effect gangland killings?

A: By spraying the victim with a rain, or hail, of bullets.

Q: Why?

A: Because of a gangster feud. Slain mobster tried to muscle in.

Q: With what is the spraying done?

A: Murder weapon; that is, a sawed-off shotgun.

Q: The spraying causes what to ring out?

A: A fusillade of shots.

Q: Which the neighbors traditionally mistake for what?

A: The sound of an auto backfiring.

Q: The sprayed mobster is in what state?

A: He is riddled with bullets, of course.

Q: Prior to succumbing to this riddling, he traditionally refuses to do what?

A: He refuses to name his assailants.

Q: Why?

A: The code of gangland, or the underworld, forbids it.

Q: Following the spraying and riddling, the killers do what?

A: They flee to a gangster hideout unless felled by cops' bullets.

Q: Splendid, Mr. Arbuthnot. Now tell us what yawns for an alleged murderer.

A: Jail. He faces the noose, or chair.

Q: How does he behave at his trial?

A: With complete unconcern, although he may collapse at the verdict, if convicted. The tabloids rather expect it of him.

Q: What kind of moves does his lawyer make?

A: Surprise moves.

Q: With what?

A: Surprise witnesses.

Q: What does the D.A. play?

A: His trump card.

Q: How many kinds of cross-examination are there?

A: Two. Grilling and searching.

Q: If convicted of murder in the first, the guilty party does what?

A: He pays the supreme penalty. He pays his debt to society.

Q: And if acquitted?

A: He begins life anew.

Q: If an erring mate and her lover are on trial for the alleged slaying of her hubby, how do they behave toward each other in the courtroom?

A: They give no sign of recognition. They are estranged.

Q: Mr. Arbuthnot, to clear up some odds and ends, where does unwed mother leave month-old babe?

A: At the door of the rectory, neatly dressed, and with a note pinned to the dress.

Q: How do holdup men employ a revolver?

A: They jam gun in side of jeweller, bank teller, girl with payroll, or wealthy socialite.

Q: In the case of the wealthy socialite, the occasion being what?

A: A gem theft.

Q: What do wealthy women wear to gem thefts?

A: A fortune in jewels. They estimate their loss at $100,000.

Q: How do gem thefts originate?

A: Spotters put the finger on gem-laden revellers in night clubs.

Q: Well, Mr. Arbuthnot, I really think we've about covered the ground—

A: Oh, I'm sorry, but I disagree with you.

Q: Yes? What have we omitted?

A: Plenty. For one thing, you failed to ask me how the handsome Lothario to whom gullible women entrust their life savings is customarily dressed.

Q: That's right, I didn't. Well, how *is* he dressed?

A: Nattily. And after his arrest it is discovered that he has four other wives in various parts of the country. He preys on women.

Q: To be sure.

A: You didn't ask me what the police refused to divulge.

Q: I do so, gladly.

A: The contents of the note. And I'd like to remind you that women who kidnap babies are frustrated mothers, that rioting prisoners traditionally hold the warden as a hostage, and that judges castigate wife beaters and reconcile estranged lovers.

Q: Mr. Arbuthnot, are the foregoing clichés, this rich mine you have so kindly uncovered for us, confined to the tabloids?

A: Not at all. The chroniclers who write the full-size journals are by no means above stealing the tabloids' thunder when it suits their purpose.

Q: Mr. Arbuthnot, thank you very much.

A: Thank *you*.

On a Slow Train

THE MIDDLE-AGED WOMAN and the lively boy boarded the New York train at Albany. We were fifteen minutes down the river before she got settled, this because of the necessity of disposing of a large number of parcels while at the same time keeping a checkrein on the little boy, who had all the docility and repose of an exceptionally frolicsome puppy. He was about four, and his companion, as it turned out, was his grandmother.

Fortunately for Grandma the coach was not crowded, so she was able to have a seat for herself and junior, and commandeer the opposite seat for such of the parcels and packages as would not fit into the luggage rack.

One of the packages got a good deal of attention from Grandma. She regarded it with solicitude and placed it in a spot on the seat opposite where she could keep an eye on it at all times. There was a good reason for this, as we occupants of the neighboring seats soon learned. The package contained eggs. It, of course, was the package the small boy particularly wanted to meddle with.

His grandmother had her hands full defending the eggs. There was never a dull moment for her on that trip. Nor, happily, for the rest of us. One of the surest ways of relieving the possible tedium of a train journey is to have aboard a lively tot in close proximity to a couple dozen eggs.

"Philip, don't touch that package . . . Philip, if you break those eggs, Grandma will . . . Philip, why *can't* you sit still and be a good little . . . Philip, you're going to knock those eggs . . . Philip, if you don't get away from those eggs, Grandma will never . . ."

So it went, Grandma threatening, pleading, coaxing, cajoling, bullying, as we rolled down the shore of Mr. Hudson's river, and every one of her words passing in one Philippian ear and out the other. The more Grandma warned him not to touch the eggs, the more he wanted to touch them. Naturally. And as the duel between youth and age waxed keener, we in the nearby seats grew more and more interested. Would Philip win, or would the Grandma-egg coalition triumph?

Philip stood on the seat beside his grandmother and struck up a conversation with a woman in the seat behind. This led to a chat between the grandmother and the woman. The grandmother said that Philip was four, going on five. The woman said that he was big for his age. So full of mischief, too, and so lively. Lively, echoed the grandmother, with a sigh of mock despair which did not quite conceal a note of fond pride. He's into everything. Keep a body busy all day long just picking up after him. The woman said, Yes, he was just at that age. Grandma said he certainly was, and grabbed the subject of the analysis just as the train rounded a curve and nearly sent him sprawling on the eggs.

Since women travellers—and men travellers, too, for that matter—like to tell other travellers where they are going and whence they have come, we learned that Grandma had been visiting her daughter on a farm in the Adirondacks, that the daughter was Philip's mother, and that Grandma was bringing Philip back to Brooklyn for a visit, to see if Brooklyn could take it.

Never, not even on an Alfred Hitchcock mystery train, has a journey had more suspense than that trip to New York from Albany. Grandma valiantly waged what at times looked like a losing battle for the eggs. It occurred to some of us innocent but interested bystanders that her problem might be simplified if she stowed the eggs in the luggage rack overhead, beyond the reach of young Genghis Khan. Somebody ventured to tell her so, but she scanned the rack dubiously. She said it was already filled and that the eggs would probably fall out if placed up there, and were on the whole safer on the seat where she could keep an eye on them—and on Philip.

There may have been another reason why Grandma did not favor putting the eggs in the rack. Possibly, without quite being aware of it, she was enjoying the conflict with Philip and did not wish a truce.

The candy butcher came along and a traveller asked Grandma if it would be all right to buy Philip a chocolate bar. She said it would, and it certainly was all right with Philip. In five minutes he had consumed a third of the bar and the other two thirds was on his face, and he had taken on the look of an end man in an old-time minstrel show. Ablutions followed, resisted stoutly by Philip until, in the middle of the washing, he fell asleep quite unexpectedly.

We felt relieved at this, for Grandma's and the eggs' sake. After a while, as the train bowled on toward Poughkeepsie, this feeling of relief was supplanted by a vague feeling that something was missing in our lives. And we realized that with Philip asleep and the eggs enjoying security, life on that train was drab. Grandma seemed affected, like the rest of us. She sighed and fidgeted. The conductor and the trainmen, who know everything that happens in their tight little domain, had very soon learned about the battle between Philip and the eggs, and had grown as interested as the passengers. They had been dropping by every so often to find out the score. The conductor was ostensibly on the side of law and order, i.e., the eggs, and, allying himself with Grandma, adjured Philip not to break them, but there was a glint in his eye that could be interpreted as a desire to be in at the crash, if Humpty-Dumpty did fall.

At Harmon, life took on new meaning again. Philip awoke, refreshed by slumber, and immediately made a pass at the eggs. Grandma countered. We all ceased fretting over whatever petty personal problems we had brought with us and resumed interest in the contest.

The last hour of the ride was full of excitement, but as we glided into the Grand Central, those who had been betting on Philip were confounded, for the eggs were unbroken. Grandma put herself between him and the eggs and got him encased in his things. A Galahad among us volunteered to help Grandma get Philip and the impedimenta to the concourse where she said her husband would be waiting. Grandma welcomed the aid, and entrusted a share of the parcels to the Galahad, but said, "I'll take care of the eggs."

She did. As we passed up the ramp toward the waiting room

a porter pushing a luggage truck bore down on us. Grandma made to sidestep him and in so doing she dropped the eggs. They went down to the cement flooring with a highly final-sounding crash.

Victory, tardy and at second-hand, failed to interest Philip. He was screaming "Grampa!" at a man advancing toward us.

Nobody but Nobody Undersells Uncle Sam

THE BARGAIN SALES are always an important and pleasant part of the post-Christmas season in New York, but I really believe this has been the most exciting winter for bargains since 1928, the year the jewellers then known as Black, Starr & Frost advertised a pearl necklace at $685,000. My, will I ever forget the crush in front of Black, Starr & Frost's the morning after that ad appeared! I bucked the scrimmage for about five minutes, then gave up.

This year, the bargain sales started off quietly enough, with the usual nice letters about sheets and pillowcases from McCutcheon's, Best's, and Altman's. The advertisements in the newspapers gave no hint of the coming excitement. The Shopping Guide in the Sunday *Times* offered for two dollars, postpaid, money-back guarantee, a dowser to use in locating spots on a wall where mirrors and pictures could be hung. I sent for one right away, because our dowser had been borrowed by someone (Kenneth Roberts, I presume) and that was the last we saw of it. From the Shopping Guide I also laid in a gross or two of ballpoint pens at ten for a dollar; some storm windows, in case of a storm; an air purifier, in case of impure air; and a Signal Corps pole-climbing outfit, in case the mood to climb a pole seized me. I further invested in a United States Army outdoor heater, as I own fifty by a hundred feet of outdoors in the rear of my home and it frequently needs heating at this time of year. A portable

153

garage at $6.75, a set of folding legs on the chance that something might turn up to fold them under, and two gallons of rust remover completed my purchases for the time being.

These were all musts—household necessities one can't well do without. The only item I thought bordered on the extravagant was the rust remover, but, as matters turned out, it was to come in mighty handy. By the time I had got that shopping done, January was well under way, yet the bargain sales indicated nothing more than the normal seasonal upswing.

It was on January 11th, when the United States Maritime Administration offered the liner President Coolidge for sale, that I first suspected this might turn out to be a winter to make a bargain hunter sit up and take notice. An ocean liner, even a used one, is a handy thing to have around, affording as it does an admirable place for the children to play on rainy afternoons. And there was a feature that made the President Coolidge an especially alluring challenge to the bargain hunter: it lies at the bottom of Espíritu Santo Harbor, in the New Hebrides, where it was sunk in 1942. Of course, a ship under water is an even more ideal place for the kids on rainy days. You simply adjust their little diving helmets and push them firmly down, down, down, out of the rain, and leave them to their romps. The drawback was that Espíritu Santo Harbor was not included in the package with the President Coolidge—and I have no harbor at the moment. I *had* a harbor, but, as usual, somebody (I think it was Herman Wouk) borrowed it, and it went the way of the dowser I loaned Kenneth Roberts, the tarpon I loaned Hemingway, and the seaweed I let Rachel Carson take.

The President Coolidge was by no means the only bargain the government offered. There were fourteen ships in all, each one safe and secure at the bottom, or on the beach, of some distant harbor. They included the Norluna, Flora MacDonald, Allan-a-Dale, Francis Asbury, George W. Norris, City of Dallas, James McNeill Whistler, Thomas T. Tucker, Zoroaster, and Alfred the Great. I figured that a shrewd bargainer could get the whole lot, F.O.B. Davy Jones' locker, for less than he would have paid for that pearl necklace. And it is worth noting that during the time when our government was offering these really amazing bargains, Gimbel's and Macy's did not even have sales on such notions as ferryboats and barges. Nobody but nobody undersells Uncle Sam.

I see I got a trifle mixed. Zoroaster and Alfred the Great got in the list of ships by mistake. They are not vessels. They are two of the heroic-size statues on the roof of the Supreme Court's Appellate Division courthouse on Madison Square. Just after the government announced the sale of the ships, the City of New York announced that it would have to get rid of the statues, because they are in the way of extensive additions planned for the courthouse. The bargain season was now really humming. Who wants a pillowcase when he can get a statue, more than lifesize, of Mahomet, Lycurgus, Moses, Confucius, Justinian, Solon, Zoroaster, or Alfred the Great? Any one of them would simply *make* a rock garden. Or a householder handy with a chisel could easily gouge a hole in Zoroaster's stomach and insert a clock there, and have something really useful as well as artistic. And just think of Justinian as a lamp!

As for the ships, it was hard to know which one to choose. I wanted them all, of course, though the government admitted that some of them had no salvageable cargo aboard. The Norluna, however, carried two hundred and fifty tons of cryolite when she was stranded on Arluk Island, Canada, and cryolite sounds like something bound to come in handy around the house sooner or later. But the Thomas T. Tucker really took my eye. She ran aground near Cape Town, South Africa, during the war, with a cargo of corrugated iron, steel rails, barbed wire, and chassis bodies.

I had been saying to myself, "I've got all this rust remover, now if I could only get hold of some rust!" And here were fourteen ships full of rust, especially the Thomas T. Tucker. What luck! Nevertheless, I realized that if I bought the ships I would have further problems. Fourteen ships would be useless unless I had a lighthouse to go with them.

As if in answer to a prayer, the government, on January 14th, offered for sale the Navesink Lighthouse, at Atlantic Highlands, New Jersey—and it is a twin lighthouse. Two of them for the price of one. What a January it was turning out to be! The *Herald Tribune,* in its account of the proposed lighthouse sale, stated that one prospective buyer had already appeared, Miss Blanche Yurka, the actress. I do not know why Miss Yurka should want a lighthouse, but I suspect that she is thinking along my lines, and has her eye not only on the twin lighthouse but on the fourteen ships, and possibly on those Appellate Division statues, too. If so, I want to serve notice on Miss Yurka right now that I intend to *get* those trinkets, and no holds barred. I have learned a few bargain-sale tricks myself since that day in 1928 when Doris Duke, Babs Hutton, and Peggy Joyce trampled on my corns and put me out of the running for that six-hundred-and-eighty-five-thousand-dollar pearl necklace, and I will not hesitate to use them.

Of course, there have been attempts to throw cold water on my enthusiasm.

"I never saw anyone like you for collecting old junk," said a person in my family. "You're worse than the Collyer brothers."

"What in heaven's name do you want with a lighthouse?" said another person.

"What does *anybody* want with a lighthouse!" I snapped. The person's remark nettled me, for it was just what well-meaning friends had said twenty years ago when I had a chance to buy Labrador. I can hear them now: "What in heaven's name do you want with Labrador?"

Well, there never was a bargain like Labrador. If I recall the circumstances, the depression was at its worst, and Newfoundland found herself hard up for cash and offered to sell the Labrador territory for $100,000,000. It was not because I heeded the advice of my bearish friends that Labrador slipped through my fingers; it was just that I couldn't swing the deal alone. I felt sure Newfoundland would take $80,000,000 cash if it was offered. I had $500. Well, money was tight, and I was unable to raise the other $79,999,500.

I do not remember who finally bought Labrador, but I imagine it was William Zeckendorf. Though it may have been Blanche Yurka. But you can see what a marvellous position I would be in today if I only had Labrador. I've got—or as good as got—fourteen fine ships. I've all but got the twin lighthouse, and I probably can get the city to sell me those statues. And I've *actually* got the rust remover.

All I need is some harbors for my ships, and if I had Labrador I'd have plenty of harbors. I've planned exactly what to do with my bargains, too. There will be a place for everything and everything in its place. I'll put two of the statues on top of the lighthouse and dispose of the others around the peninsula at spots that need brightening up. Everything will be put to good use, even the cryolite, when I make sure what it is.

"Collyer brothers" indeed!

The Passing of the Old Front Porch

ILL FARES THE land, to hastening ills a prey, where wealth accumulates and front porches decay. Anyone who was brought up in a house with a front porch knows this, and anyone brought up in such a house who has had to live in a house without a front porch knows it even better. In Europe they have never gone in for the front porch as we know it in America. And look at the shape Europe is in today. In Manhattan they gave up front porches years ago because land got too valuable. And look at Manhattan today.

The front porch is an American institution of high civic and moral value. It is a sign that the people who sit on it are ready and willing to share the community life of their block with their neighbors. It performs the useful function of enabling a neighbor to keep track of what the other neighbors are doing, and vice versa. In the block where I live we know more about each other's affairs in the summer when we move out to the front porch than we do in the winter when we sit in the parlor and look at television, and I claim that my neighbors' affairs are far more interesting than any television show I've seen thus far.

If anyone at this point says, "What's he beefing about? Nobody has cast any reflections on front porches!" my answer is, "Yes, they have." Maybe not in words, but actions speak louder than words; and there is a deplorable tendency afoot in this country to snoot the front porch of our forefathers; to give it, as the poet so aptly phrased it, the bum's rush. I don't want to put the finger on anyone but I think it's the architects who are to blame. They are trying to persuade home builders, in the interest of aesthetics, to build homes with no front porches, or with token front porches which are as bad as no front porch at all; chaste, arched, fantail doorways with a bricked step as a "porch" hardly big enough for the newspaper boy to throw the evening paper at, and hit. One of the good points about the old-fashioned front porch was that even when his pitching arm was off the newspaper boy was sure to land the paper *somewhere* on the porch, out of reach of rain and snow. If the front porch goes, our Fourth Estate will get soggier and soggier, especially during wet spells.

These designers who are trying to make the fronts of houses look more Colonial by slicing off the front porches may not realize it but they are practically undermining democracy. The Pilgrims had no front porches on their salt-box houses because they had no time to sit on front porches. They were too busy pulling up stumps, listening to Cotton Mather twice on Sunday, and conquering the Indians who had some kind of foolish notion that they owned New England just because they were there first. Why, those redskins didn't even know it was *called* New England until the Pilgrim fathers told them.

Not until Custer finally defeated the Indians did this nation get enough leisure to sit on the front porch in the cool of the evening and pipe off what the neighbors were up to. And now we want to throw away that priceless heritage, that Fifth Freedom.

The front porch has been as effective a medium for the exchange of community ideas as the town meeting or the cracker barrel. Presidents have been elected on front porches. Defeated there too, probably. The first thing a Presidential nominee's managers do after the convention is to take pictures of him sitting on his front porch in a rocking chair, being homespun and folksy; or accepting the nomination (which is called "bowing to the will of the people") from behind the Dutchman's Pipe vine. A good rambling front porch is worth 3,000,000 votes to a candidate, but it must ramble. A porch is no good unless it rambles. And the homespun states like Ohio, Indiana and Massachusetts are as good as lost to a candidate if he hasn't got a front porch. Of course a candidate with a porch isn't as fortunate as one who was born in a log cabin, but Presidents who were born in log cabins are hard to find nowadays. The nearest approach we have now to the log cabin is the ranch-type bungalow, but I do not expect to live to vote for the first President born in a ranch-type bungalow.

Householders who refuse to have front porches on their homes are subconsciously shirking the chore of getting the porch furniture up from the basement in April and dusting it off; or they don't want to go to the trouble of putting up the flower boxes.

You cannot, of course, have a front porch without flower boxes, filled with geraniums, with a smattering of petunias and fuchsias, and a lambrequin of ivy vines drooping over the sides. The function of the flower box is very important in any well-regulated, liberally beporched, neighborly block. At nine o'clock in the morning, after the youngsters have been got off to school or day camp, all the ladies come out, aproned, and bearing watering cans. This gives them a chance not only to water the geraniums but to pass the time of day with each other, exchange the news, comment on same, and find out if anything sensational has happened to anybody overnight. It is a much pleasanter way of finding out what's going on than by telephoning, which is what the girls have to do in winter; at least in the morning, for the bridge clubs do not meet until afternoon.

The front porch keeps on being useful all day long in one way or another and it really comes into its own on an evening in the dog days when everyone foregathers on it. The neighbors come over and visit your front porch, or you go over and visit their porch. It is the forum for the exchange of much valuable data on the weather; remarks like "Looks as though it's clouding up for rain" or "Hot day tomorrow. Look at that sunset." Gardens are discussed, also politics on local, state, national, international and cosmic levels, and the fate of the universe settled.

One of the veranda's functions has undoubtedly declined. In the Booth Tarkington era young folks used to do their courting on the porch in the hammock, the family tactfully vacating the porch on such occasions. That was where Gentle Julia and George Ade's belles held court for bewitched young men, and listened to the lovelorn suitors play the mandolin. But there is no denying that the automobile has dealt the porch a setback in the department of love. Nevertheless I remain unconvinced that an engagement that has blazed up in a convertible has as good a chance of survival as one that was sparked in a porch swing. Look at your statistics on divorce.

Occasional householders, while succumbing to the craze to slice off the front porch, soothe their consciences by switching the porch to the rear of the house, claiming this gives them more privacy. Who wants privacy on a front stoop? It was invented so that folks could escape privacy, often just another name for monotony. That alibi won't do, fellow homebuilders. The place for a porch is in the front and one that is in the rear should stick to its original, and honorable, function, namely, to serve as a repository for the morning milk, and a storage place for rakes, hoes, lawn mowers, catcher's mitts, bats, old laundry, abandoned paint brushes, broken-down kiddie cars and other familiar impedimenta of the American home. It won't do to put the front porch on the side of the house, either, nor on top of the house, in case any architect is thinking of going to that extremity. A front porch on top of a house automatically becomes a fixture known as a widow's walk, and a widow's walk is at home nowhere except on a house in a New England seaport town. A front porch is a front porch—but I begin to sound like Gertrude Stein in her *"Tender Buttons"* period, and that way madness lies.

Another thing: if the front porch goes, the rocking chair will go, too. The twain are inseparable. The rocking chair is as essential a fixture of the front porch as the jardiniere filled with maidenhair ferns, and the soothing art of rocking has reached its greatest flower on the American front porch. It is significant that the most accomplished rockers are little children and elderly people, for it is well known that these two age groups are the wisest people in the country; and that citizens in the age brackets between ten and fifty years are immature, impetuous, usually deficient in judgment, and seldom given to rocking. Little children like to rock at breakneck speed, endangering life and limb all over the porch, but the old folks have learned the wisdom of rocking placidly as they knit, or gossip, or size up the new television set being delivered to the folks across the way. ("Now tell me, how can *they* afford a television set? Why I hear he wasn't able to meet the payment on his mortgage last fall!")

Let us think twice before we give the good old front porch of our ancestors the gate. True, some concessions to modern taste could be made. For instance, if the porch is of the General Grant period the fancy scrollwork could be stripped off and nobody, or nothing, would be any the worse except the sparrows that like to roost in the interstices of the scrollwork. But let us keep the basic structure of the fine old institution intact.

That's Real Good of You

NOT LONG AGO, I went to the attic to look for an old scrapbook but found, hidden behind a trunk, a basket filled with old snapshots: a record of family and friends, of high jinks and carefree capers that dated back as far as four decades. Of course, I forgot the scrapbook and spent the rest of the day looking over the basket collection.

"Who's the Mack Sennett character here, with the bathing pants halfway down to his ankles?" I asked the Aged Relative.

"Why, that's you," she said. "Nantasket Beach in 1916. Don't you remember?"

I sighed, took up another picture, and chuckled.

"Oh, look at Floradora here. Get the cast-iron pompadour, and that alarm clock pinned to her chest."

"It was not an alarm clock," said the Aged R. haughtily. "It was a chatelaine watch. I got it for Christmas. They were the rage that year. And what's the matter with the pompadour?"

I switched quickly to another exhibit, a very faded snapshot of seven little boys with seven little sleds. The little boys wore toboggan caps pulled down to their eyes and sweaters yanked up to their noses, so they had a kind of veiled, oriental aspect. I remembered that occasion quite well. We were sliding down the hill in Greenridge Cemetery one cold day, and a neighbor came along and took our picture. One of the seven little boys is now with a great industrial company, one is a cop, one is a butcher, two are dead, one is me, and I have lost track of the seventh.

Up came a snapshot of myself taken with an old pal—Bill, an elephant of great friendliness and personality. I knew him twenty-five years ago when I had a newspaper assignment that would make any small boy pant to be a reporter. I covered the Ringling Circus when it was at the old Madison Square Garden. In the same category was an autographed photograph of the intelligent and charming lady who honored the Ringling side show in those days as the Armless Wonder. She wrote a neat Spencerian hand with her toes and read Proust with the Bearded Lady.

The snapshots in the basket collection represent amateur photography in days when the art was free and untrammelled, high, wide, and handsome, catch-as-catch-can, and devil take the hindmost. The hind-most was the fellow who got into the picture late and had to stand behind the girl wearing the Merry Widow hat, so all you see of him is an ear.

In those days, no editor dreamed of giving two pages in his Sunday edition to the activities of amateur photographers. If you saw an impertinent kitten slapping a patient mastiff with her paw, you smiled and walked on; but today a snapshot of that endearing tableau might get you a $500 prize for "Cutest Animal Picture of the Year." I saw in a recent Sunday paper that there's a new contest afoot, with $60,000 to be awarded in prizes. Monsieur Daguerre started something when he invented photography 110 years ago.

Any time a sociable crowd gathered, the moment was sure to come when someone said, "Let's take some pictures." A rush for the best positions followed, and I seem to recall they were usually won by the coy exhibitionists who protested, "Oh, you don't want *me* in it" and "No, no, not me. I take a terrible picture." There was always a camera fiend willing and anxious to snap the pictures, but most of us wanted to be on the other side of the camera. The lens addicts outnumbered the camera fiends at least a hundred to one. The rate has diminished since prize money appeared.

Whoever was selected to snap the pictures instantly grew very bossy, placed everybody so they were effectively blinded by the sun, and started barking brisk commands: "For crying out loud, George, smile! You look as if you were going to a funeral. Bill, put your arm around Laura. Joe, get closer to Sue. A little more to the center,

Peggy. Look up, Maggie. Where's Emma? Somebody get Emma. I want her in it."

Then the boss fiddled importantly with the box camera for ten minutes, while all the subjects asked him to get a move on, did he want to keep us standing there all day. Finally he said, "All right now, hold still everybody"—at which three people moved. He clicked the shutter, and it was all over. Then Emma ran up, crying, "Aw, gee, why didn't you tell me you were taking pictures?"

The snapshot Turned Out Good or it Turned Out Bad; but even if it Turned Out Good, the attempt to smile as we squinted into the full majesty of the sun gave most of us the expression of one who sees the dentist approaching with the drill.

I couldn't possibly remember who snapped the pictures in my collection. None of them was Steichen, but they brought a refreshing enthusiasm, an almost manic ardor to their task, and their work has a devil-may-care quality that I'm not sure I'd want to exchange for the polished efforts of today's camera-contest prize winners.

The snapshot taken the day I graduated from college, for example—I doubt if it would take a prize today, yet it has a certain charm. In cap and gown, I am seated on the running board of an open car. Four relatives and friends are inside the automobile. But I am in the auto, too, as a kind of ectoplasmic manifestation through which the four are visible. And I think that's me at the extreme left of the film, though it may be only a smudge from the developer's thumb. The four friends and relatives also are on the running board with me, and I am visible through them, so everybody gets a break and nobody can complain of discrimination.

Yet that snapshot might qualify for a prize today, at that. Not so long ago, I saw some photographs, in the very latest impressionistic manner, of Jean Cocteau in various poses: Jean floating through the air, surrounded by ectoplasm; Jean superimposed on a photograph of his own soul; Jean shaking hands with arms that had no bodies. Essentially, I insist, my graduation snapshot is in the same class. Both pictures are double-double exposures.

In the basket collection, there is one snapshot I wish had been thrown out. It shows a group of four, two skirted and two in trousers. Presumably, two are men and two are women; but I can't prove that, because somebody jiggled the photographer's arm the moment he snapped the picture, with the result that he photographed only the lower half of the group. Who are they? I don't know. The Aged R. can't say, either. It's tantalizing. I lost fully half an hour's sleep over the matter. Maybe one is the missing Judge Crater, or the long-lost Dorothy Arnold.

Having a picture taken informally brought out the pixie in a surprising number of subjects, caused capers and pranks in people who never dreamed of cutting up at other times. I have a snapshot, taken in 1918, of a treasured girl friend in her brother's sailor uniform. I have a snapshot of a college chum in the frock he wore as leading lady of a college play. Looks cute, too. Lest anyone think there is no mote in my eye, I admit instantly that I found a snapshot of myself taken with a girl for whom I had an eternal passion during our senior year in high school. I am wearing her hat, and she is wearing mine. Mine was a derby, the first and last derby I ever owned. I wonder what became of that derby. I wonder what became of the girl.

I noticed two interesting points about the basket collection. There are few babies in it, and almost no snow. Today babies play a highly important role in the camera industry. Prize-contest judges, who are almost sure to have been babies once themselves, are pushovers for a cute baby picture, such as one of an intrepid mite trying to insert his head into the jaws of that same good-natured mastiff that took so much lip from the fresh kitten. But in the old days, in the rush to get in the front row when someone cried, "Let's take some pictures," there was no nonsense about babies first. Apparently, only the huskier, more determined infants got into the picture. The others found themselves behind the fellow behind the girl wearing the Merry Widow hat.

There cannot be more than a foot and a half of snow in the three hundred snapshots in my collection, though many of them were taken in an Adirondack town in wintertime. Snow wasn't a treat to us. But now people get prizes for artistic snapshots of snow. During each winter week, a handsome award is copped by a lyric photograph of a brook rippling between banks piled high with beautiful, fresh-fallen snow; usually the picture's title is "Winter" or "January" or "Can Spring Be Far Behind?" My advice to an amateur camera fiend seeking his fortune is to get himself a baby, either philoprogenitively or by borrowing; but if he cannot do that, let him take to the woods, anchor at a brook, and wait for a heavy snowfall. His fortune will be made—unless he runs into an open winter.

Basing my statements on the law of averages and an analysis of my basket collection, I will now make a few guesses. I guess that if you have a basket or an album of old snapshots, it contains a picture of yourself or friends in a fake airplane at Coney Island, or some other amusement park.

Also, you have a snapshot taken on the steps of a high school. Your arm is around the boy, or girl, of your dreams, who married somebody else and is now stout and a grandparent.

You have a snapshot, which astounds you, of a tiny lad of four or five, a neighbor or relative, who is now halfback on his college eleven, or was a hero in the war, and stands six feet three in his socks: "For Pete's sake, don't tell me that's Bob!"

You have snapshots of yourself or cronies on vacation trips. The mania for taking snapshots always reached its height during travel. The snapshots were mailed home with witty comments: "The one on the left is the Washington Monument, not Lillian. Love. Stanley."

You have a snapshot of a grey blur. It might be London in a fog, but the writing on it states, "This is the beach. Our cottage is over there at the left behind the big pine. Note the dock where we go swimming from." Landscapes invariably baffled the amateur photographers of old. Landscapes never moved, or didn't move much, but somehow they always managed to come out blurred.

Let's see, what else—oh, you must have a snapshot of a brother or an old flame, showing subject and roommate in their chambers at college. They're at their desks boning for an exam, or trying to make you think they are. The wall reveals a wealth of college pennants and some pin-up girls. The pin-up girls at the time I am thinking of were Pearl White and Beverly Bayne. Subject and roomie are smoking class pipes.

You have the usual snapshots of yourself or loved ones in uniform. The sailor brother standing beside, and apparently on best terms with, a Buddha in some far-off land, or atop a camel beside the Pyramids, or feeding the pigeons at St. Mark's.

You have snapshots of class reunions, weddings, galas, all the merry, carefree moments of yore happily petrified in gelatin for you to sigh over years later. You have no gloomy snapshots. At sad moments, nobody got out the camera and shouted, "Let's take some pictures." Though I do have one picture of a wake. A group of a hundred men and women, newspaper folk, were photographed the night of the last edition of a beloved newspaper, which had been sold and absorbed into another journal. We are all laughing and seemingly carefree, though for most of us the coach was due to turn into a pumpkin at the stroke of midnight.

Let's Take a Few Wooden Nickels

ON LEAVING A young neighbor after we had watched a basketball game together, I was seized by an antic impulse and said, "So long, Jimmy. Don't take any wooden nickels now." To my surprise, he received the ancient crack with pleasure, as if it were something new and sparkling in raillery; and not long afterward, I heard him urging one of his contemporaries not to take any wooden nickels.

To one who cast his first vote for Woodrow Wilson, it was consoling to know that this badinage of yesteryear had a charm for the youth of today. Who knows? Maybe it could be dusted off and put into circulation again. I'm not sure it hasn't got everything the slang of today has; I might be sure if I only knew what the slang of today has.

The advice about wooden nickels was only one of several gay parting phrases formerly in vogue. Use of them stamped you as a card, a caution, and a clip. You could bid a friend farewell by telling him you'd see him in the funny sheet, or you could say, "So long. Don't do anything I wouldn't do." It was considered rakish to say, "Goodbye. If you can't be good, be careful." And there was always the breezy farewell "Olive oil!" which, I believe, was supposed to be a comical rendering of "*Au revoir.*" Hot diggety dog, those were the days!

During the regime of William Howard Taft, there was a wealth of folk repartee with which a fellow could prove himself a humdinger. You had to talk fast, though, for the repartee was open stock, and your cronies had as ready access to it as you had.

The same is true today, but I suspect there is less choice today than there was two score years ago. On the rare occasions when I try to match wits—unsuccessfully—with the younger set, about the only blistering comeback I can summon is "Oh, yeah?" I use it because it sounds up to date; but next time I bandy repartee with a stripling, I may see if I can't confound him with some of the antique comebacks. I'll tell him to go 'way back and sit down. I'll tell him to put an egg in his shoe and beat it, or beat it while his shoes are good. Or I'll say, "Go home and tell your mother she wants you." Those shafts used to be considered quite crushing. If all else fails, I can run the gamut of the Go School: "Go paddle your canoe." "Go roll your hoop." "Go soak your head." "Go sell your papers." "Go lay an egg." "Go chase yourself." "Go sit on a tack." "Go hire a hall." You see? I've mentioned twelve ways of saying "Twenty-three, skidoo!" and haven't begun to skim the surface. In fact, I forgot a good one: "Shoo-fly, you bother me!"

Observe the wealth of imagery in these rowdy injunctions. Why, they almost amount to poetry. Contrast them with "Scram!" which is about all the harassed youth of today can think to say when he wants someone to go away. "Scram!" I submit, is overdoing the laconic. I blame this trend on the mad pace of modern life and the poetry of T. S. Eliot.

It was not only important not to be kidded, but it was essential not to admit you were vulnerable to kidding. Naturally, you didn't want to be classed as a boob and have your friends say you didn't know enough to come in out of the rain, or that you were so dumb you thought Rex Beach was a summer resort. Therefore, you had to remind wise guys that your mother did not have any foolish children. You asked them who they thought they were stringing. Stringing meant jollying. Ribbing is the word for it today. You urged them to get hep to themselves, and you said "Aw, pull your head in. Don't be a clam all your life."

There were lots of ways to jeer at a friend. Most of them have given way to "Oh, yeah!" You could restrain overexuberant cronies by saying, "You tell 'em, cabbage. You've got the head." Or you could put them in their places by such mocking ripostes as "Say not so!" "How can you be so cruel?" "Wouldn't that jar you?" "Whodathunk it?" "Wouldn't that get your goat?" "Ain't that rich?" "Can you beat it?" "Quitcher kidding!" You asked them to tell it to Sweeney or the Marines, and you begged them not to be Airedales.

In the days of the Merry Widow hat, boys were funnier than girls. Boys were expected to be cutups. Girls were supposed to laugh at the boys' antics, or pretend to be shocked.

Persiflage abounded at high-school spreads and similar saturnalia. On shaking hands with a girl, you might wow her with "Pardon my wet glove" or "Slip me five, kiddo." We were greatly concerned about two girls named Ann and Mabel: constantly wanted to know how old Ann was, and were incessantly curious to find out if Mabel didn't think it was awful. We devastated pals at the ice-cream parlors and other hot spots by asking if they had seen Arthur. Arthur who? Our thermometer. End of joke. Or, have you seen Benny? Benny who? Albany. Oh, we were the ones! We advised one another not to make love in a potato patch. Give up? Because potatoes have eyes. Cornfields were out, too, because corn has ears. Never tell a horse anything: horses carry tails. Time flies. You can't; they go too fast. Ah, we had a million of 'em. There was a vogue for a tiny gadget called the chestnut bell. You pinned it on a friend when he told a stale joke, like any of the above, or like the one about the quickest way to spread news. What was that? Telephone, telegraph, telewoman. Is that so, Mr. Smarty?

If you wished to reflect on a friend's mental powers, and very often you did, you told him he was dippy or bughouse. There was nobody home in his belfry except the bats. It was stylish to say "Ishkabibble" instead of "I should worry"; but if you wanted to be real fancy, you chanted, "I should worry, I should fret, I should marry a suffragette." (Variation: I should worry, I should care, I should marry a millionaire.) There was a spate of parodies on "Hiawatha," a catchy ballad that swept the forty-five states and the three territories of Oklahoma, New Mexico and Arizona just after the start of this rambunctious century. "Did the lady of the river have a sliver—" Ah, but it's no good unless you hear it sung.

We divided friends into categories: lemons, pills, boobs, wise guys, buttinskis, dumb Doras, and so on. In the adolescent set, a pretty girl was a lulu, a pip, a peacherino, a darb, or a lallapaloosa—in short, some punkins. A fast worker made goo-goo eyes at a lallapaloosa and complimented her with such honeyed phrases as, "Ah, there, good-lookin', you take the cake." "Where you been all my life?" "You're the candy kid. You're out of sight." He told her she was just what the doctor ordered and that he'd leave his happy home for her. If the lallapaloosa fell for this mullarkey, they spooned. But in the privacy of their vestal *Kaffeeklatschs*, the lallapaloosa's girl friends said to one another enviously, "Pooh, she'd fall for anything with pants on."

The bashful type of male did not have such easy command of this kind of raillery. Only the sheiks were versed in it. A sheik was a lounge-lizard or a handsome Harry.

If the friend wore a new hat—lads wore hats in the days I am recalling—the conventional compliments were "Pipe the lid" or "Where did you get that hat?" If he wore his trousers ankle-length, you asked him if it was raining in London; and if he had just had a haircut, you asked him who hit him with the ax. When a newcomer joined a gathering, it was smart to compliment him by saying, "Look what the cat brought in!" Anything you liked was the cat's pajamas or, for variety, the cat's meow, and anything you disapproved of was applesauce, banana oil, or hooey.

All this was the wit of the sophisticated high-school set. The grade-school set had its own, even more rudimentary, wit. If a new boy appeared on the block, it was necessary to put him in his place. As soon as he cast his first glance in your direction, you challenged him by yelling, "Rubber!" If he was half a man, and he was, he retorted, "Stretch it!" and your answer to that was "Throw it up an' ketch it!" After that, probably you and he became friends and you had your first fight.

Then, as now, arguments among boys were loud, but not so violent as they sounded. Candid disparagement was the rule. The short and ugly word was passed frequently, but it hardly ever brought on physical combat. When a boy said, "You're a liar," honor was satisfied if you retorted, "You're another," and he then countered with "You're his brother."

In moments when he was out of patience with me, usually several times a day, Charlie, a close friend of mine, was fond of telling me that my face would fry an onion. That charge never upset me too much, because I knew that in moments of stress, Charlie told all his fellow choirboys and his two sisters that their faces had this odd property. Anyhow, his compliment gave me a chance to remind him that *his* face would stop a clock. From there, the dialogue might go on as follows:

CHARLIE: Aw, you're full o' prunes.
ME: Ah, gowan. You think you're the only pebble on the beach.
CHARLIE: Ah, gowan. You're off your trolley.
ME: Aw, you think you're the whole thing.
CHARLIE: Aw, gowan. You're full o' banana oil.

Protocol, stipulated those introductory growls, "ah" and "aw"; "gowan" could be added or not, as the speaker's caprice dictated.

I still have a hard time to keep from crying "Bread an' butter!" when, in walking, a tree gets between me and a companion. *Keep* from saying it? I *say* it. It's bad luck if you don't. And if I should ever visit the old swimming hole again, I'm sure that as we kids start to strip, I'll cry, "Last one in's a rotten egg!"

It was important to catch the last glimpse of a friend on parting from him after an evening of playing cops and robbers. I don't know whether this was a local rite, peculiar to our town, or whether all boys everywhere practised it. You darted a look at your companion, turned away quickly, cried, "Saw your face last!" and scooted into your house. Or you tapped him, cried, "Last touch!" and then ran for it. It took a lot of maneuvering to see a face last or gain last touch, and the game was often prolonged until a parent came to the door and ordered one of the contestants inside to bed.

Little girls were fond of teasing boys by chanting a jingle that went something like this: *Joe is mad and I am glad and I know what to please him. A bottle o' wine to make him shine and Alice May to squeeze him.* Alice May (or whoever) could be a damsel to whom Joe was precociously vulnerable, or she could be one he particularly disliked. Usually, if Joe was nine or ten, she was the latter. I have wondered how the odd "Rubaiyat" note of the wine got into so innocent a rhyme.

Well, friends, I have to go in the house now and do my homework. Saw your face last!

Letter to a Neighbor

Dᴇᴀʀ Bᴜᴛᴄʜ—

After you went home this afternoon, I fell into a pensive mood and found myself taking stock of our friendship and what it has meant to me since that memorable day when we first met. Truly, it has been a tonic to know you. You have been a stimulating, even a galvanizing, influence. You have made it necessary for me to ponder a new set of values—a chore that can be unsettling at my age.

Do you recall the circumstances of our first meeting? Well, I do. It was a year ago. You had just moved to our block, and you were sitting on your front-porch steps, reconnoitering the neighborhood. I came along with an armful of groceries. You pulled a gun on me and cried, "Stick 'em up! I gotcha covered. What's your name?" I told you. Then you asked if I knew *your* name, and without waiting for my answer, you told me, and added that you were four years old, going on five. Then you escorted me the remaining fifty yards to my home. I did not know until you informed me later that there were bears and tigers in the block and that they might have hyjacked my groceries and menaced my person. It was mighty friendly of you, pardner, to escort me home under armed guard that day. It marked the beginning of a friendship during which I have been held up at the point of a gun several times a day, answered about a hundred thousand questions, and learned quite a lot.

Yours is the most scientific mind I have ever encountered. If I had

your curiosity, energy and perseverance, Butch, with my experience, I'd have long since discovered a way to put the atom back
together again, minding its own business and doing nobody harm.

You weigh each statement on its merits. You let nothing go un-
challenged. I soon realized the hazard of making rash remarks in
your presence. There was that day in our kitchen when I was host
at our customary midafternoon snack. I had just turned out what I
thought was a pretty good job of a peanut-butter sandwich, and I
handed it to you, saying gaily, "Try that on your zither, squirt."

You said, "What's a zither, Frank?"

I sensed I had made a strategic error and pretended not to hear
your question, so you said again, "What's a zither?"

It was useless to dodge the issue. My back was to the wall. I tried to
explain to you what a zither was, and under your cross-examination,
I realized how little I really knew about zithers. Yet I had thought I
knew all I needed to know about them, for mine has been, on the
whole, a zitherless life.

There was the morning I went downstairs to breakfast and found
you waiting to keep me company, a neighborly act that has frequently enlivened my morning meal and has done much to give the
day a cheerful start. I coughed, and explained that I had a frog in
my throat.

You demanded to see the frog. You asked how it got in my throat.
And why. And when. Thinks I, An up-to-date psychiatrist would answer this tot's questions honestly and not try to duck the issue or fill
him with evasions that might confuse his thinking in later life. He
should be told that a frog in the throat is only a figure of speech. But
if I had told you any such thing, you would have wanted to know
what a figure of speech was, and that way, I knew, madness lay. For
weeks after that morning, you made daily demands that I produce
the frog from my throat. Truly, it has been said—or, rather, is being
said by me right now—that elephants and little boys never forget.

You have transformed gardening from the sedative chore of a
middle-aged gaffer into an adventure fraught with the unpredict-
able. Every blossom in the garden, every blade on the sward, trem-
bles when you gallop into view, joyfully crying that you have come
to help me weed. And every weed rejoices. There is some consola-
tion in the fact that your range of interests is so wide and you are
so busy a man that you cannot spare any one matter your attention

for more than two minutes. But in those two minutes, you can help a petunia into a state of advanced debility.

No gardener ever had a more willing apprentice than you. A spirit of scientific inquiry pervades all your activities, though I must admit that the afternoon you sat on the sprinkler to find out how it feels to sit on a sprinkler did neither the sprinkler nor your clean suit any good. Your project to catch squirrels and place them in a large paper bag was original, and it was no fault of yours that the squirrels wouldn't co-operate. That day you decided to tame a bee in a bottle, how were you to know that bees prefer to live in hives and have a very effective means of argument against being placed in bottles? And someday I hope to convince you that the birdbath really does not need to be refilled every five minutes. Birds are not that particular, even though you like to squirt a hose.

On the more constructive side, I think you have really thrown a scare into what you refer to as the Japaneetles. I can believe that word has gone out among them that a young Attila is helping Old Man Sullivan these days, and that the area is not healthy for Japaneetles.

I once read that one must never say "Don't!" to a child, because of the frustrating effects of that word. Something gentler, more persuasive, and less staccato, like "Oh, I wouldn't do that if I were you" was recommended. Well, Butch, as you know, I have tried telling you that I wouldn't do that if I were you on occasions when you were fiddling with the knobs on the gas stove and toying with the Aged Relative's collection of fragile glass knickknacks. I found this warning about as effective as saying, "Tut, tut! I wouldn't if I were you!" to a descending bolt of lightning.

Begging the pardon of the child-guidance experts, I have come to the conclusion that there are occasions in dealing with healthy small boys when "Don't!" or even *"Don't!"* is the only practical command. And I doubt if the moderate amount of "Don'ting" you get on your visits to Sullivan Grange is going to damage as healthy an ego as yours, for I recall the Sunday when you showed up in shining new raiment, I said, "Why, Butch, you're just about the handsomest fellow I ever saw." And you said, "I know it." Ah, Narcissus, admire yourself while you may. You won't be able to go through life very long as candidly as that. Like the rest of us, you'll learn to dissemble.

It must be great fun to be your age and discover something new almost every day. Words, for instance. Jawbreakers appear quite casually in your budding vocabulary; they're taken from the-Lord-knows-what conversations among your elders and calculated to astonish the unwary. I recall the snowy day when I cautioned you to stay clear of the eaves because of possible avalanches from the roof, and you reassured me, saying, "That's all right, Frank. I'm not allergic to snow." By the way, I'm glad you call me "Frank." It elevates me to comradeship with you on a basis of equality, just as though I, too, were four, going on five.

Why shouldn't I treasure you? You regard me as an oracle and a paragon—well, almost a paragon—and you are the only one who does. You are flatteringly and overwhelmingly interested in everything I do or plan to do. I make no move without hearing, "What are you going to do now, Frank?" . . . "Why?" . . . "What are you doing that for, Frank?" . . . "Why?" . . . "Where are you going, Frank? Can I go, too?" . . . "Why can't I?"

I have learned a lot from you, too. I have become, to my considerable surprise, well versed in the small, personal duties of valet and nursemaid, heretofore entirely out of my line. When you are taking your leave on a winter afternoon, I can button you into your Things with a fair degree of skill, if the Aged R. isn't on hand to do it more skillfully. Your shoelaces come untied every ten minutes, on a timetable as dependable as Old Faithful's. I have learned to tie them. And I remember the small panic that seized me the first time you clambered into my lap (a lap that up to that moment had been undented by any form as small as yours) and demanded that I tell you a story.

This afternoon you were Into Everything. You tried to turn up the thermostat as high as it would go, to see what would happen. The glass *objets d'art* were in mortal peril several times. You were "Don'ted" generously, and finally, when you asked if you might listen to Hoppy, I was only too glad to turn on the television, to keep you quiet. But when ten minutes had gone by, the silence in the living room, save for Hoppy's gunfire, was so marked as to be ominous. I went to the door and peered in the room, to see what was cooking.

You were fast asleep in the big armchair. The recent dynamo was just a tired little boy, worn out by the arduous duties of running the neighborhood and seeing to it that no dull moments crept therein. You looked so small and so innocent, curled up in the armchair, that an odd emotion came over me.

Can it be that you have made me discontented with my status in life? Before I met you, I was a contented bachelor.

"It Seems There Were—"

WHENEVER POSSIBLE I have sat at the feet of wise men to try to learn something, and now in the fullness of my span I am sure of only two things: I know that if a man licks an envelope flap hastily he will certainly cut his tongue, and I know that if a man buttonholes me and says, "Here's a story that'll kill you," it won't kill me at all—but it *may* leave me in the same state of moody depression that seized Queen Victoria the time she said, "We are not amused."

They do not always say, "This one'll kill you." Sometimes they say, "This'll hand you a laugh." But it seldom does. The few successful anecdote dispensers I know never guarantee or oversell their wares, and they never, not even hardly ever, grasp the other fellow by the lapel or back him against a wall. Oral humor ought to be dispensed from a minimum distance of three feet. People rarely like to be breathed on, especially by an overenthusiastic raconteur, and seldom relish the view of the latter's tonsils which is afforded when he laughs immoderately at his own joke.

I always seem to be on the receiving end of funny stories. It is a bitter pill for one who would like to tell a joke as well as the next. I too would like to shine. I too yearn to startle social gatherings into awed admiration, like the young man in the advertisement who broke into French when nobody dreamed he had it in him.

Yet there are bugs in my anecdote technique that seem to bar me from being the life of the party. Either I can't remember a funny story, or I remember all of it except the point, or I remember the point too but get it wrong. These are no mean faults in one aspiring to scintillate. I have tried to remedy them. On hearing a good story I have slipped from the room to jot down the gist of it, but later, when I fish the memo out, I haven't any idea what it means.

It has happened, albeit seldom, that friends have given me that heart-warming accolade, the invitation to tell a funny story. "Oh, Frank, tell that wonderful story you told the other night at Gwen's, the one about the penguin and the tax collector." So, if I can recall it, I launch gallantly into the one about the tax collector and the penguin—after just enough affectation of reluctance to establish modesty without prompting anyone to say, "Well, don't tell it if you really don't want to." Just as I am creeping up on the point of the tale, an interloper bursts into our circle and shouts, "Hey, break it up, folks, we're all going to play The Game." Or he says, "Say, listen to this one Harry just told me; it'll kill you."

I do not think a few taps from the bastinado or a slight dunking in boiling oil would be too unfair a retaliation on such point killers. Am I unjust?

Well, if I cannot be prince of raconteurs, I can demand perfection in more successful rivals. For years I have been waging a cold war on a friend who is an inveterate joke teller but cheats at it. In the middle of his stories he makes a long pause. This causes his hearers to assume that the joke is over, and that the point is something so subtle and sophisticated that it is not even visible. Since most people would rather die than be caught not being sophisticated, his hearers laugh riotously and vow they never heard anything so rare. My friend then gives them a patient, injured look and starts on the second twenty minutes of his anecdote, and are their faces red! He planned it that way; he does it to tease them.

After falling for his ruse a few times, I determined he would not make a chump of me again, and he hasn't. We spend whole evenings together, mainly in silence, I waiting for his mid-joke pause to end, and he hoping I will laugh in the wrong place. I think I have him bothered.

Another friend goes even farther. He not only pauses in midstream but walks away from me, hoping by that maneuver to trick me into laughing before the joke is over. I fell for it a few times, too, but now when he walks away I follow. No matter where he goes, I go. Upstairs, downstairs, in my lady's chamber, after him I go, Ruth to his Naomi, bloodhound to his Eliza, Sullivan to his Gilbert, Perrin to his Lea. I don't mind. I'm fond of walking. Often take long hikes. I'll track him over Mount Everest before I let him get away with his scurvy trick.

Raconteuring needs regulation. Jokes and funny stories should be told only by masters of the art. Good raconteurs are born. So, unfortunately, are bad raconteurs. There are probably not more than three hundred master raconteurs in the country today. Three hundred is really a large quota when you consider that there are only ten jokes in the world, each one of which renews itself every twenty years.

A license should be required of raconteurs before they are allowed to practice raconteuring, and a careful screening should precede the granting of the licenses. We might even establish an academy for promising young raconteurs, to take over when the veteran raconteurs have been retired on account of laughing too many citizens to death.

Funny stories are dynamite in the hands of the amateur and the telling of them is habit-forming unless the character is strong. A man hears a story, laughs at it, and passes it on to his friends. Every time he waylays a pal and retells it, he laughs harder—but he does not notice that often his pal does not laugh at all, especially if, as frequently occurs, our hero has told the pal that story several times. Drugged by his own mirth, the unfortunate man comes to believe that the mantle of Mark Twain has descended upon him and that he is the first raconteur of his time. Nothing so astonishing as this hallucination exists in this country.

I know a man who is in the grip of the story-telling habit. Once he was able to conduct his share of an ordinary conversation without difficulty, but he has long since reached a point where if a telephone operator happens to say, "Number, please?" he says, "Say-y, that reminds me of a story." He lives in a world of fantasy peopled by a couple of Irishmen named Pat and Mike and other characters from Joe Miller's joke book. When he enters a room, people come from far and wide to get away from him. Even wasps at the kill sting their prey into a merciful coma before devouring them, but this chap forces his victims to listen to his stories without any anesthesia whatever. Some day when he buttonholes a friend and says, "Here's one that'll kill you," the shoe is going to be on the other foot, and *he* will be the corpse. It will be too bad, for he is a good husband and kind father. At least he was until a year ago, when his wife left him, naming Joe Miller as corespondent.

In licensing raconteurs, we must debar from practice all those displaying certain ominous symptoms. For instance, the Lama Mahoney would be debarred. Poor fellow, he developed the rash habit of prefacing all his stories with "Have you heard the one about . . ." and his friends, grown desperate, developed the habit of answering "Yes" and walking away. He brooded about this quite a bit, lost considerable weight, and at length, in a misanthropic and embittered frame of mind, left to join a monastery in Tibet.

None shall be granted a license who sins the sin of the Lama Mahoney, or who says, "Stop me if you've heard this one." Has anyone who *has* heard this one ever stopped anyone who said, "Stop me if you've heard this one"? Not very often. People are basically kind and will wrench their diaphragms to work up a fake laugh over a joke they have heard before. And before, and before.

Nobody who says, "I can't tell it the way George tells it" shall be permitted to matriculate in our academy for yarn spinners. If he cannot tell it as well as George tells it, then we must send for George and let *him* tell it. We must be cruel in order to be kind. There is no room for the timid or the apologetic in the ruthless give and take of the anecdote mart.

No ancient mariners in the academy either, please. They are the fellows gifted with a sure and malign instinct for waylaying the unwary with their jokes just at the moment when the unwary is on his way to a wedding feast, or to catch a train, and is late. The ancient mariners' stories never take less than twenty minutes to tell.

There will also be an embargo on the wishful thinker who says, "Emma has heard me tell this one before, but she won't mind if I tell it again." But Emma does mind. She is too polite to say so, but she *will* mind.

We must have no truck with that hapless type who goes haywire at parties, after he has eaten his third stalk of celery stuffed with Roquefort. You know him. At the inevitable moment he blurts eagerly, "I heard a story at the office the other day but"—glancing gallantly at the ladies—"I'm not sure whether I dare tell it in mixed company." The ladies say politely, "Why nonsense, go right ahead and tell it. We're broad-minded." So he does, and it turns out that he was right in the first place, and that it is not a story for mixed company; and a silence as of the tomb descendeth upon the multitude, and the hapless one looketh in vain for an orifice in the floor wherein he may creep and hide for ever and ever.

I predict there will be few applications from women for raconteur licenses. Women are not commonly given to spinning yarns or telling funny stories. They are too smart. They have heard their menfolk at it. Little girls do not spin funny yarns either, but little boys laugh inordinately at the corniest jokes and delight in the most bloodcurdling puns. The child is father to the man.

Shall we debar the teller of comical stories in dialect? There is a strong bloc which demands that this be done, or they will filibuster. I don't know. Certainly we must be adamant about the fellow who tells a joke in what he no doubt honestly believes, and indeed announces, to be an Irish brogue, but which comes out Swedish. And we must in self-defense put our foot down in the case of the raconteur who prides himself on his mastery of, let us say, an Italian dialect which to the baffled ears of his audience resembles a mixture of Southern Alabamian, Jewish, and German dialects, with one of the less common patois used by the Incas of Peru thrown in to make it harder.

A CATALOG OF SELECTED
DOVER BOOKS
IN ALL FIELDS OF INTEREST

5 X 5

A CATALOG OF SELECTED DOVER
BOOKS IN ALL FIELDS OF INTEREST

CONCERNING THE SPIRITUAL IN ART, Wassily Kandinsky. Pioneering work by father of abstract art. Thoughts on color theory, nature of art. Analysis of earlier masters. 12 illustrations. 80pp. of text. 5⅜ × 8½.　　　　23411-8 Pa. $3.95

ANIMALS: 1,419 Copyright-Free Illustrations of Mammals, Birds, Fish, Insects, etc., Jim Harter (ed.). Clear wood engravings present, in extremely lifelike poses, over 1,000 species of animals. One of the most extensive pictorial sourcebooks of its kind. Captions. Index. 284pp. 9 × 12.　　　　23766-4 Pa. $12.95

CELTIC ART: The Methods of Construction, George Bain. Simple geometric techniques for making Celtic interlacements, spirals, Kells-type initials, animals, humans, etc. Over 500 illustrations. 160pp. 9 × 12. (USO)　　　　22923-8 Pa. $9.95

AN ATLAS OF ANATOMY FOR ARTISTS, Fritz Schider. Most thorough reference work on art anatomy in the world. Hundreds of illustrations, including selections from works by Vesalius, Leonardo, Goya, Ingres, Michelangelo, others. 593 illustrations. 192pp. 7⅛ × 10¼.　　　　20241-0 Pa. $9.95

CELTIC HAND STROKE-BY-STROKE (Irish Half-Uncial from "The Book of Kells"): An Arthur Baker Calligraphy Manual, Arthur Baker. Complete guide to creating each letter of the alphabet in distinctive Celtic manner. Covers hand position, strokes, pens, inks, paper, more. Illustrated. 48pp. 8¼ × 11.

24336-2 Pa. $3.95

EASY ORIGAMI, John Montroll. Charming collection of 32 projects (hat, cup, pelican, piano, swan, many more) specially designed for the novice origami hobbyist. Clearly illustrated easy-to-follow instructions insure that even beginning papercrafters will achieve successful results. 48pp. 8¼ × 11.　　　　27298-2 Pa. $2.95

THE COMPLETE BOOK OF BIRDHOUSE CONSTRUCTION FOR WOOD-WORKERS, Scott D. Campbell. Detailed instructions, illustrations, tables. Also data on bird habitat and instinct patterns. Bibliography. 3 tables. 63 illustrations in 15 figures. 48pp. 5¼ × 8½.　　　　24407-5 Pa. $1.95

BLOOMINGDALE'S ILLUSTRATED 1886 CATALOG: Fashions, Dry Goods and Housewares, Bloomingdale Brothers. Famed merchants' extremely rare catalog depicting about 1,700 products: clothing, housewares, firearms, dry goods, jewelry, more. Invaluable for dating, identifying vintage items. Also, copyright-free graphics for artists, designers. Co-published with Henry Ford Museum & Green-field Village. 160pp. 8¼ × 11.　　　　25780-0 Pa. $9.95

HISTORIC COSTUME IN PICTURES, Braun & Schneider. Over 1,450 costumed figures in clearly detailed engravings—from dawn of civilization to end of 19th century. Captions. Many folk costumes. 256pp. 8⅜ × 11¾.　　　　23150-X Pa. $11.95

STICKLEY CRAFTSMAN FURNITURE CATALOGS, Gustav Stickley and L. & J. G. Stickley. Beautiful, functional furniture in two authentic catalogs from 1910. 594 illustrations, including 277 photos, show settles, rockers, armchairs, reclining chairs, bookcases, desks, tables. 183pp. 6½ × 9¼. 23838-5 Pa. $9.95

AMERICAN LOCOMOTIVES IN HISTORIC PHOTOGRAPHS: 1858 to 1949, Ron Ziel (ed.). A rare collection of 126 meticulously detailed official photographs, called "builder portraits," of American locomotives that majestically chronicle the rise of steam locomotive power in America. Introduction. Detailed captions. xi + 129pp. 9 × 12. 27393-8 Pa. $12.95

AMERICA'S LIGHTHOUSES: An Illustrated History, Francis Ross Holland, Jr. Delightfully written, profusely illustrated fact-filled survey of over 200 American lighthouses since 1716. History, anecdotes, technological advances, more. 240pp. 8 × 10¾. 25576-X Pa. $11.95

TOWARDS A NEW ARCHITECTURE, Le Corbusier. Pioneering manifesto by founder of "International School." Technical and aesthetic theories, views of industry, economics, relation of form to function, "mass-production split" and much more. Profusely illustrated. 320pp. 6⅛ × 9¼. (USO) 25023-7 Pa. $9.95

HOW THE OTHER HALF LIVES, Jacob Riis. Famous journalistic record, exposing poverty and degradation of New York slums around 1900, by major social reformer. 100 striking and influential photographs. 233pp. 10 × 7⅞. 22012-5 Pa $10.95

FRUIT KEY AND TWIG KEY TO TREES AND SHRUBS, William M. Harlow. One of the handiest and most widely used identification aids. Fruit key covers 120 deciduous and evergreen species; twig key 160 deciduous species. Easily used. Over 300 photographs. 126pp. 5⅜ × 8½. 20511-8 Pa. $3.95

COMMON BIRD SONGS, Dr. Donald J. Borror. Songs of 60 most common U.S. birds: robins, sparrows, cardinals, bluejays, finches, more—arranged in order of increasing complexity. Up to 9 variations of songs of each species. Cassette and manual 99911-4 $8.95

ORCHIDS AS HOUSE PLANTS, Rebecca Tyson Northen. Grow cattleyas and many other kinds of orchids—in a window, in a case, or under artificial light. 63 illustrations. 148pp. 5⅜ × 8½. 23261-1 Pa. $4.95

MONSTER MAZES, Dave Phillips. Masterful mazes at four levels of difficulty. Avoid deadly perils and evil creatures to find magical treasures. Solutions for all 32 exciting illustrated puzzles. 48pp. 8¼ × 11. 26005-4 Pa. $2.95

MOZART'S DON GIOVANNI (DOVER OPERA LIBRETTO SERIES), Wolfgang Amadeus Mozart. Introduced and translated by Ellen H. Bleiler. Standard Italian libretto, with complete English translation. Convenient and thoroughly portable—an ideal companion for reading along with a recording or the performance itself. Introduction. List of characters. Plot summary. 121pp. 5¼ × 8½. 24944-1 Pa. $2.95

TECHNICAL MANUAL AND DICTIONARY OF CLASSICAL BALLET, Gail Grant. Defines, explains, comments on steps, movements, poses and concepts. 15-page pictorial section. Basic book for student, viewer. 127pp. 5⅜ × 8½. 21843-0 Pa. $4.95

BRASS INSTRUMENTS: Their History and Development, Anthony Baines. Authoritative, updated survey of the evolution of trumpets, trombones, bugles, cornets, French horns, tubas and other brass wind instruments. Over 140 illustrations and 48 music examples. Corrected and updated by author. New preface. Bibliography. 320pp. 5⅜ × 8½. 27574-4 Pa. $9.95

HOLLYWOOD GLAMOR PORTRAITS, John Kobal (ed.). 145 photos from 1926–49. Harlow, Gable, Bogart, Bacall; 94 stars in all. Full background on photographers, technical aspects. 160pp. 8⅜ × 11¼. 23352-9 Pa. $11.95

MAX AND MORITZ, Wilhelm Busch. Great humor classic in both German and English. Also 10 other works: "Cat and Mouse," "Plisch and Plumm," etc. 216pp. 5⅜ × 8½. 20181-3 Pa. $5.95

THE RAVEN AND OTHER FAVORITE POEMS, Edgar Allan Poe. Over 40 of the author's most memorable poems: "The Bells," "Ulalume," "Israfel," "To Helen," "The Conqueror Worm," "Eldorado," "Annabel Lee," many more. Alphabetic lists of titles and first lines. 64pp. 5³⁄₁₆ × 8¼. 26685-0 Pa. $1.00

SEVEN SCIENCE FICTION NOVELS, H. G. Wells. The standard collection of the great novels. Complete, unabridged. First Men in the Moon, Island of Dr. Moreau, War of the Worlds, Food of the Gods, Invisible Man, Time Machine, In the Days of the Comet. Total of 1,015pp. 5⅜ × 8½. (USO) 20264-X Clothbd. $29.95

AMULETS AND SUPERSTITIONS, E. A. Wallis Budge. Comprehensive discourse on origin, powers of amulets in many ancient cultures: Arab, Persian, Babylonian, Assyrian, Egyptian, Gnostic, Hebrew, Phoenician, Syriac, etc. Covers cross, swastika, crucifix, seals, rings, stones, etc. 584pp. 5⅜ × 8½. 23573-4 Pa. $12.95

RUSSIAN STORIES/PYCCKNE PACCKA3bI: A Dual-Language Book, edited by Gleb Struve. Twelve tales by such masters as Chekhov, Tolstoy, Dostoevsky, Pushkin, others. Excellent word-for-word English translations on facing pages, plus teaching and study aids, Russian/English vocabulary, biographical/critical introductions, more. 416pp. 5⅜ × 8½. 26244-8 Pa. $8.95

PHILADELPHIA THEN AND NOW: 60 Sites Photographed in the Past and Present, Kenneth Finkel and Susan Oyama. Rare photographs of City Hall, Logan Square, Independence Hall, Betsy Ross House, other landmarks juxtaposed with contemporary views. Captures changing face of historic city. Introduction. Captions. 128pp. 8¼ × 11. 25790-8 Pa. $9.95

AIA ARCHITECTURAL GUIDE TO NASSAU AND SUFFOLK COUNTIES, LONG ISLAND, The American Institute of Architects, Long Island Chapter, and the Society for the Preservation of Long Island Antiquities. Comprehensive, well-researched and generously illustrated volume brings to life over three centuries of Long Island's great architectural heritage. More than 240 photographs with authoritative, extensively detailed captions. 176pp. 8¼ × 11. 26946-9 Pa. $14.95

NORTH AMERICAN INDIAN LIFE: Customs and Traditions of 23 Tribes, Elsie Clews Parsons (ed.). 27 fictionalized essays by noted anthropologists examine religion, customs, government, additional facets of life among the Winnebago, Crow, Zuni, Eskimo, other tribes. 480pp. 6⅛ × 9¼. 27377-6 Pa. $10.95

FRANK LLOYD WRIGHT'S HOLLYHOCK HOUSE, Donald Hoffmann. Lavishly illustrated, carefully documented study of one of Wright's most controversial residential designs. Over 120 photographs, floor plans, elevations, etc. Detailed perceptive text by noted Wright scholar. Index. 128pp. 9¼ × 10¾.
27133-1 Pa. $11.95

THE MALE AND FEMALE FIGURE IN MOTION: 60 Classic Photographic Sequences, Eadweard Muybridge. 60 true-action photographs of men and women walking, running, climbing, bending, turning, etc., reproduced from rare 19th-century masterpiece. vi + 121pp. 9 × 12. 24745-7 Pa. $10.95

1001 QUESTIONS ANSWERED ABOUT THE SEASHORE, N. J. Berrill and Jacquelyn Berrill. Queries answered about dolphins, sea snails, sponges, starfish, fishes, shore birds, many others. Covers appearance, breeding, growth, feeding, much more. 305pp. 5¼ × 8¼. 23366-9 Pa. $7.95

GUIDE TO OWL WATCHING IN NORTH AMERICA, Donald S. Heintzelman. Superb guide offers complete data and descriptions of 19 species: barn owl, screech owl, snowy owl, many more. Expert coverage of owl-watching equipment, conservation, migrations and invasions, etc. Guide to observing sites. 84 illustrations. xiii + 193pp. 5⅜ × 8½. 27344-X Pa. $8.95

MEDICINAL AND OTHER USES OF NORTH AMERICAN PLANTS: A Historical Survey with Special Reference to the Eastern Indian Tribes, Charlotte Erichsen-Brown. Chronological historical citations document 500 years of usage of plants, trees, shrubs native to eastern Canada, northeastern U.S. Also complete identifying information. 343 illustrations. 544pp. 6½ × 9¼. 25951-X Pa. $12.95

STORYBOOK MAZES, Dave Phillips. 23 stories and mazes on two-page spreads: Wizard of Oz, Treasure Island, Robin Hood, etc. Solutions. 64pp. 8¼ × 11.
23628-5 Pa. $2.95

NEGRO FOLK MUSIC, U.S.A., Harold Courlander. Noted folklorist's scholarly yet readable analysis of rich and varied musical tradition. Includes authentic versions of over 40 folk songs. Valuable bibliography and discography. xi + 324pp. 5⅜ × 8½. 27350-4 Pa. $7.95

MOVIE-STAR PORTRAITS OF THE FORTIES, John Kobal (ed.). 163 glamor, studio photos of 106 stars of the 1940s: Rita Hayworth, Ava Gardner, Marlon Brando, Clark Gable, many more. 176pp. 8⅜ × 11¼. 23546-7 Pa. $11.95

BENCHLEY LOST AND FOUND, Robert Benchley. Finest humor from early 30s, about pet peeves, child psychologists, post office and others. Mostly unavailable elsewhere. 73 illustrations by Peter Arno and others. 183pp. 5⅜ × 8½.
22410-4 Pa. $5.95

YEKL and THE IMPORTED BRIDEGROOM AND OTHER STORIES OF YIDDISH NEW YORK, Abraham Cahan. Film Hester Street based on Yekl (1896). Novel, other stories among first about Jewish immigrants on N.Y.'s East Side. 240pp. 5⅜ × 8½. 22427-9 Pa. $6.95

SELECTED POEMS, Walt Whitman. Generous sampling from *Leaves of Grass*. Twenty-four poems include "I Hear America Singing," "Song of the Open Road," "I Sing the Body Electric," "When Lilacs Last in the Dooryard Bloom'd," "O Captain! My Captain!"—all reprinted from an authoritative edition. Lists of titles and first lines. 128pp. 5³⁄₁₆ × 8¼. 26878-0 Pa. $1.00

THE BEST TALES OF HOFFMANN, E. T. A. Hoffmann. 10 of Hoffmann's most important stories: "Nutcracker and the King of Mice," "The Golden Flowerpot," etc. 458pp. 5⅜ × 8½. 21793-0 Pa. $8.95

FROM FETISH TO GOD IN ANCIENT EGYPT, E. A. Wallis Budge. Rich detailed survey of Egyptian conception of "God" and gods, magic, cult of animals, Osiris, more. Also, superb English translations of hymns and legends. 240 illustrations. 545pp. 5⅜ × 8½. 25803-3 Pa. $11.95

FRENCH STORIES/CONTES FRANÇAIS: A Dual-Language Book, Wallace Fowlie. Ten stories by French masters, Voltaire to Camus: "Micromegas" by Voltaire; "The Atheist's Mass" by Balzac; "Minuet" by de Maupassant; "The Guest" by Camus, six more. Excellent English translations on facing pages. Also French-English vocabulary list, exercises, more. 352pp. 5⅜ × 8½. 26443-2 Pa. $8.95

CHICAGO AT THE TURN OF THE CENTURY IN PHOTOGRAPHS: 122 Historic Views from the Collections of the Chicago Historical Society, Larry A. Viskochil. Rare large-format prints offer detailed views of City Hall, State Street, the Loop, Hull House, Union Station, many other landmarks, circa 1904–1913. Introduction. Captions. Maps. 144pp. 9⅜ × 12¼. 24656-6 Pa. $12.95

OLD BROOKLYN IN EARLY PHOTOGRAPHS, 1865–1929, William Lee Younger. Luna Park, Gravesend race track, construction of Grand Army Plaza, moving of Hotel Brighton, etc. 157 previously unpublished photographs. 165pp. 8⅞ × 11¾. 23587-4 Pa. $13.95

THE MYTHS OF THE NORTH AMERICAN INDIANS, Lewis Spence. Rich anthology of the myths and legends of the Algonquins, Iroquois, Pawnees and Sioux, prefaced by an extensive historical and ethnological commentary. 36 illustrations. 480pp. 5⅜ × 8½. 25967-6 Pa. $8.95

AN ENCYCLOPEDIA OF BATTLES: Accounts of Over 1,560 Battles from 1479 B.C. to the Present, David Eggenberger. Essential details of every major battle in recorded history from the first battle of Megiddo in 1479 B.C. to Grenada in 1984. List of Battle Maps. New Appendix covering the years 1967–1984. Index. 99 illustrations. 544pp. 6½ × 9¼. 24913-1 Pa. $14.95

SAILING ALONE AROUND THE WORLD, Captain Joshua Slocum. First man to sail around the world, alone, in small boat. One of great feats of seamanship told in delightful manner. 67 illustrations. 294pp. 5⅜ × 8½. 20326-3 Pa. $5.95

ANARCHISM AND OTHER ESSAYS, Emma Goldman. Powerful, penetrating, prophetic essays on direct action, role of minorities, prison reform, puritan hypocrisy, violence, etc. 271pp. 5⅜ × 8½. 22484-8 Pa. $5.95

MYTHS OF THE HINDUS AND BUDDHISTS, Ananda K. Coomaraswamy and Sister Nivedita. Great stories of the epics; deeds of Krishna, Shiva, taken from puranas, Vedas, folk tales; etc. 32 illustrations. 400pp. 5⅜ × 8½. 21759-0 Pa. $9.95

BEYOND PSYCHOLOGY, Otto Rank. Fear of death, desire of immortality, nature of sexuality, social organization, creativity, according to Rankian system. 291pp. 5⅜ × 8½. 20485-5 Pa. $8.95

A THEOLOGICO-POLITICAL TREATISE, Benedict Spinoza. Also contains unfinished Political Treatise. Great classic on religious liberty, theory of government on common consent. R. Elwes translation. Total of 421pp. 5⅜ × 8½. 20249-6 Pa. $8.95

MY BONDAGE AND MY FREEDOM, Frederick Douglass. Born a slave, Douglass became outspoken force in antislavery movement. The best of Douglass' autobiographies. Graphic description of slave life. 464pp. 5⅜ × 8½. 22457-0 Pa. **$8.95**

FOLLOWING THE EQUATOR: A Journey Around the World, Mark Twain. Fascinating humorous account of 1897 voyage to Hawaii, Australia, India, New Zealand, etc. Ironic, bemused reports on peoples, customs, climate, flora and fauna, politics, much more. 197 illustrations. 720pp. 5⅜ × 8½. 26113-1 Pa. **$15.95**

THE PEOPLE CALLED SHAKERS, Edward D. Andrews. Definitive study of Shakers: origins, beliefs, practices, dances, social organization, furniture and crafts, etc. 33 illustrations. 351pp. 5⅜ × 8½. 21081-2 Pa. **$8.95**

THE MYTHS OF GREECE AND ROME, H. A. Guerber. A classic of mythology, generously illustrated, long prized for its simple, graphic, accurate retelling of the principal myths of Greece and Rome, and for its commentary on their origins and significance. With 64 illustrations by Michelangelo, Raphael, Titian, Rubens, Canova, Bernini and others. 480pp. 5⅜ × 8½. 27584-1 Pa. **$9.95**

PSYCHOLOGY OF MUSIC, Carl E. Seashore. Classic work discusses music as a medium from psychological viewpoint. Clear treatment of physical acoustics, auditory apparatus, sound perception, development of musical skills, nature of musical feeling, host of other topics. 88 figures. 408pp. 5⅜ × 8½. 21851-1 Pa. **$9.95**

THE PHILOSOPHY OF HISTORY, Georg W. Hegel. Great classic of Western thought develops concept that history is not chance but rational process, the evolution of freedom. 457pp. 5⅜ × 8½. 20112-0 Pa. **$9.95**

THE BOOK OF TEA, Kakuzo Okakura. Minor classic of the Orient: entertaining, charming explanation, interpretation of traditional Japanese culture in terms of tea ceremony. 94pp. 5⅜ × 8½. 20070-1 Pa. **$3.95**

LIFE IN ANCIENT EGYPT, Adolf Erman. Fullest, most thorough, detailed older account with much not in more recent books, domestic life, religion, magic, medicine, commerce, much more. Many illustrations reproduce tomb paintings, carvings, hieroglyphs, etc. 597pp. 5⅜ × 8½. 22632-8 Pa. **$10.95**

SUNDIALS, Their Theory and Construction, Albert Waugh. Far and away the best, most thorough coverage of ideas, mathematics concerned, types, construction, adjusting anywhere. Simple, nontechnical treatment allows even children to build several of these dials. Over 100 illustrations. 230pp. 5⅜ × 8½. 22947-5 Pa. **$7.95**

DYNAMICS OF FLUIDS IN POROUS MEDIA, Jacob Bear. For advanced students of ground water hydrology, soil mechanics and physics, drainage and irrigation engineering, and more. 335 illustrations. Exercises, with answers. 784pp. 6⅛ × 9¼. 65675-6 Pa. **$19.95**

SONGS OF EXPERIENCE: Facsimile Reproduction with 26 Plates in Full Color, William Blake. 26 full-color plates from a rare 1826 edition. Includes "The Tyger," "London," "Holy Thursday," and other poems. Printed text of poems. 48pp. 5¼ × 7. 24636-1 Pa. **$4.95**

OLD-TIME VIGNETTES IN FULL COLOR, Carol Belanger Grafton (ed.). Over 390 charming, often sentimental illustrations, selected from archives of Victorian graphics—pretty women posing, children playing, food, flowers, kittens and puppies, smiling cherubs, birds and butterflies, much more. All copyright-free. 48pp. 9¼ × 12¼. 27269-9 Pa. **$5.95**

PERSPECTIVE FOR ARTISTS, Rex Vicat Cole. Depth, perspective of sky and sea, shadows, much more, not usually covered. 391 diagrams, 81 reproductions of drawings and paintings. 279pp. 5⅜ × 8½. 22487-2 Pa. $6.95

DRAWING THE LIVING FIGURE, Joseph Sheppard. Innovative approach to artistic anatomy focuses on specifics of surface anatomy, rather than muscles and bones. Over 170 drawings of live models in front, back and side views, and in widely varying poses. Accompanying diagrams. 177 illustrations. Introduction. Index. 144pp. 8⅜ × 11¼. 26723-7 Pa. $8.95

GOTHIC AND OLD ENGLISH ALPHABETS: 100 Complete Fonts, Dan X. Solo. Add power, elegance to posters, signs, other graphics with 100 stunning copyright-free alphabets: Blackstone, Dolbey, Germania, 97 more—including many lower-case, numerals, punctuation marks. 104pp. 8⅛ × 11. 24695-7 Pa. $8.95

HOW TO DO BEADWORK, Mary White. Fundamental book on craft from simple projects to five-bead chains and woven works. 106 illustrations. 142pp. 5⅜ × 8. 20697-1 Pa. $4.95

THE BOOK OF WOOD CARVING, Charles Marshall Sayers. Finest book for beginners discusses fundamentals and offers 34 designs. "Absolutely first rate . . . well thought out and well executed."—E. J. Tangerman. 118pp. 7¾ × 10⅝. 23654-4 Pa. $5.95

ILLUSTRATED CATALOG OF CIVIL WAR MILITARY GOODS: Union Army Weapons, Insignia, Uniform Accessories, and Other Equipment, Schuyler, Hartley, and Graham. Rare, profusely illustrated 1846 catalog includes Union Army uniform and dress regulations, arms and ammunition, coats, insignia, flags, swords, rifles, etc. 226 illustrations. 160pp. 9 × 12. 24939-5 Pa. $10.95

WOMEN'S FASHIONS OF THE EARLY 1900s: An Unabridged Republication of "New York Fashions, 1909," National Cloak & Suit Co. Rare catalog of mail-order fashions documents women's and children's clothing styles shortly after the turn of the century. Captions offer full descriptions, prices. Invaluable resource for fashion, costume historians. Approximately 725 illustrations. 128pp. 8⅜ × 11¼. 27276-1 Pa. $11.95

THE 1912 AND 1915 GUSTAV STICKLEY FURNITURE CATALOGS, Gustav Stickley. With over 200 detailed illustrations and descriptions, these two catalogs are essential reading and reference materials and identification guides for Stickley furniture. Captions cite materials, dimensions and prices. 112pp. 6½ × 9¼. 26676-1 Pa. $9.95

EARLY AMERICAN LOCOMOTIVES, John H. White, Jr. Finest locomotive engravings from early 19th century: historical (1804–74), main-line (after 1870), special, foreign, etc. 147 plates. 142pp. 11⅜ × 8¼. 22772-3 Pa. $10.95

THE TALL SHIPS OF TODAY IN PHOTOGRAPHS, Frank O. Braynard. Lavishly illustrated tribute to nearly 100 majestic contemporary sailing vessels: Amerigo Vespucci, Clearwater, Constitution, Eagle, Mayflower, Sea Cloud, Victory, many more. Authoritative captions provide statistics, background on each ship. .190 black-and-white photographs and illustrations. Introduction. 128pp. 8⅞ × 11¾. 27163-3 Pa. $13.95

EARLY NINETEENTH-CENTURY CRAFTS AND TRADES, Peter Stockham (ed.). Extremely rare 1807 volume describes to youngsters the crafts and trades of the day: brickmaker, weaver, dressmaker, bookbinder, ropemaker, saddler, many more. Quaint prose, charming illustrations for each craft. 20 black-and-white line illustrations. 192pp. 4⅝ × 6. 27293-1 Pa. $4.95

VICTORIAN FASHIONS AND COSTUMES FROM HARPER'S BAZAR, 1867–1898, Stella Blum (ed.). Day costumes, evening wear, sports clothes, shoes, hats, other accessories in over 1,000 detailed engravings. 320pp. 9⅜ × 12¼.
22990-4 Pa. $13.95

GUSTAV STICKLEY, THE CRAFTSMAN, Mary Ann Smith. Superb study surveys broad scope of Stickley's achievement, especially in architecture. Design philosophy, rise and fall of the Craftsman empire, descriptions and floor plans for many Craftsman houses, more. 86 black-and-white halftones. 31 line illustrations. Introduction. 208pp. 6½ × 9¼. 27210-9 Pa. $9.95

THE LONG ISLAND RAIL ROAD IN EARLY PHOTOGRAPHS, Ron Ziel. Over 220 rare photos, informative text document origin (1844) and development of rail service on Long Island. Vintage views of early trains, locomotives, stations, passengers, crews, much more. Captions. 8⅞ × 11¾. 26301-0 Pa. $13.95

THE BOOK OF OLD SHIPS: From Egyptian Galleys to Clipper Ships, Henry B. Culver. Superb, authoritative history of sailing vessels, with 80 magnificent line illustrations. Galley, bark, caravel, longship, whaler, many more. Detailed, informative text on each vessel by noted naval historian. Introduction. 256pp. 5⅜ × 8½. 27332-6 Pa. $6.95

TEN BOOKS ON ARCHITECTURE, Vitruvius. The most important book ever written on architecture. Early Roman aesthetics, technology, classical orders, site selection, all other aspects. Morgan translation. 331pp. 5⅜ × 8½. 20645-9 Pa. $8.95

THE HUMAN FIGURE IN MOTION, Eadweard Muybridge. More than 4,500 stopped-action photos, in action series, showing undraped men, women, children jumping, lying down, throwing, sitting, wrestling, carrying, etc. 390pp. 7⅞ × 10⅝. 20204-6 Clothbd. $24.95

TREES OF THE EASTERN AND CENTRAL UNITED STATES AND CANADA, William M. Harlow. Best one-volume guide to 140 trees. Full descriptions, woodlore, range, etc. Over 600 illustrations. Handy size. 288pp. 4½ × 6⅜.
20395-6 Pa. $5.95

SONGS OF WESTERN BIRDS, Dr. Donald J. Borror. Complete song and call repertoire of 60 western species, including flycatchers, juncoes, cactus wrens, many more—includes fully illustrated booklet. Cassette and manual 99913-0 $8.95

GROWING AND USING HERBS AND SPICES, Milo Miloradovich. Versatile handbook provides all the information needed for cultivation and use of all the herbs and spices available in North America. 4 illustrations. Index. Glossary. 236pp. 5⅜ × 8½. 25058-X Pa. $6.95

BIG BOOK OF MAZES AND LABYRINTHS, Walter Shepherd. 50 mazes and labyrinths in all—classical, solid, ripple, and more—in one great volume. Perfect inexpensive puzzler for clever youngsters. Full solutions. 112pp. 8⅛ × 11.
22951-3 Pa. $4.95

PIANO TUNING, J. Cree Fischer. Clearest, best book for beginner, amateur. Simple repairs, raising dropped notes, tuning by easy method of flattened fifths. No previous skills needed. 4 illustrations. 201pp. 5⅜ × 8½. 23267-0 Pa. $5.95

A SOURCE BOOK IN THEATRICAL HISTORY, A. M. Nagler. Contemporary observers on acting, directing, make-up, costuming, stage props, machinery, scene design, from Ancient Greece to Chekhov. 611pp. 5⅜ × 8½. 20515-0 Pa. $11.95

THE COMPLETE NONSENSE OF EDWARD LEAR, Edward Lear. All nonsense limericks, zany alphabets, Owl and Pussycat, songs, nonsense botany, etc., illustrated by Lear. Total of 320pp. 5⅜ × 8½. (USO) 20167-8 Pa. $6.95

VICTORIAN PARLOUR POETRY: An Annotated Anthology, Michael R. Turner. 117 gems by Longfellow, Tennyson, Browning, many lesser-known poets. "The Village Blacksmith," "Curfew Must Not Ring Tonight," "Only a Baby Small," dozens more, often difficult to find elsewhere. Index of poets, titles, first lines. xxiii + 325pp. 5⅜ × 8¼. 27044-0 Pa. $8.95

DUBLINERS, James Joyce. Fifteen stories offer vivid, tightly focused observations of the lives of Dublin's poorer classes. At least one, "The Dead," is considered a masterpiece. Reprinted complete and unabridged from standard edition. 160pp. 5³⁄₁₆ × 8¼. 26870-5 Pa. $1.00

THE HAUNTED MONASTERY and THE CHINESE MAZE MURDERS, Robert van Gulik. Two full novels by van Gulik, set in 7th-century China, continue adventures of Judge Dee and his companions. An evil Taoist monastery, seemingly supernatural events; overgrown topiary maze hides strange crimes. 27 illustrations. 328pp. 5⅜ × 8½. 23502-5 Pa. $7.95

THE BOOK OF THE SACRED MAGIC OF ABRAMELIN THE MAGE, translated by S. MacGregor Mathers. Medieval manuscript of ceremonial magic. Basic document in Aleister Crowley, Golden Dawn groups. 268pp. 5⅜ × 8½. 23211-5 Pa. $8.95

NEW RUSSIAN-ENGLISH AND ENGLISH-RUSSIAN DICTIONARY, M. A. O'Brien. This is a remarkably handy Russian dictionary, containing a surprising amount of information, including over 70,000 entries. 366pp. 4½ × 6⅛. 20208-9 Pa. $9.95

HISTORIC HOMES OF THE AMERICAN PRESIDENTS, Second, Revised Edition, Irvin Haas. A traveler's guide to American Presidential homes, most open to the public, depicting and describing homes occupied by every American President from George Washington to George Bush. With visiting hours, admission charges, travel routes. 175 photographs. Index. 160pp. 8¼ × 11. 26751-2 Pa. $10.95

NEW YORK IN THE FORTIES, Andreas Feininger. 162 brilliant photographs by the well-known photographer, formerly with *Life* magazine. Commuters, shoppers, Times Square at night, much else from city at its peak. Captions by John von Hartz. 181pp. 9¼ × 10¾. 23585-8 Pa. $12.95

INDIAN SIGN LANGUAGE, William Tomkins. Over 525 signs developed by Sioux and other tribes. Written instructions and diagrams. Also 290 pictographs. 111pp. 6⅛ × 9¼. 22029-X Pa. $3.50

ANATOMY: A Complete Guide for Artists, Joseph Sheppard. A master of figure drawing shows artists how to render human anatomy convincingly. Over 460 illustrations. 224pp. 8⅜ × 11¼. 27279-6 Pa. $10.95

MEDIEVAL CALLIGRAPHY: Its History and Technique, Marc Drogin. Spirited history, comprehensive instruction manual covers 13 styles (ca. 4th century thru 15th). Excellent photographs; directions for duplicating medieval techniques with modern tools. 224pp. 8⅜ × 11¼. 26142-5 Pa. $11.95

DRIED FLOWERS: How to Prepare Them, Sarah Whitlock and Martha Rankin. Complete instructions on how to use silica gel, meal and borax, perlite aggregate, sand and borax, glycerine and water to create attractive permanent flower arrangements. 12 illustrations. 32pp. 5⅜ × 8½. 21802-3 Pa. $1.00

EASY-TO-MAKE BIRD FEEDERS FOR WOODWORKERS, Scott D. Campbell. Detailed, simple-to-use guide for designing, constructing, caring for and using feeders. Text, illustrations for 12 classic and contemporary designs. 96pp. 5⅜ × 8½. 25847-5 Pa. $2.95

OLD-TIME CRAFTS AND TRADES, Peter Stockham. An 1807 book created to teach children about crafts and trades open to them as future careers. It describes in detailed, nontechnical terms 24 different occupations, among them coachmaker, gardener, hairdresser, lacemaker, shoemaker, wheelwright, copper-plate printer, milliner, trunkmaker, merchant and brewer. Finely detailed engravings illustrate each occupation. 192pp. 4⅝ × 6. 27398-9 Pa. $4.95

THE HISTORY OF UNDERCLOTHES, C. Willett Cunnington and Phyllis Cunnington. Fascinating, well-documented survey covering six centuries of English undergarments, enhanced with over 100 illustrations: 12th-century laced-up bodice, footed long drawers (1795), 19th-century bustles, 19th-century corsets for men, Victorian "bust improvers," much more. 272pp. 5⅜ × 8¼. 27124-2 Pa. $9.95

ARTS AND CRAFTS FURNITURE: The Complete Brooks Catalog of 1912, Brooks Manufacturing Co. Photos and detailed descriptions of more than 150 now very collectible furniture designs from the Arts and Crafts movement depict davenports, settees, buffets, desks, tables, chairs, bedsteads, dressers and more, all built of solid, quarter-sawed oak. Invaluable for students and enthusiasts of antiques, Americana and the decorative arts. 80pp. 6½ × 9¼. 27471-3 Pa. $7.95

HOW WE INVENTED THE AIRPLANE: An Illustrated History, Orville Wright. Fascinating firsthand account covers early experiments, construction of planes and motors, first flights, much more. Introduction and commentary by Fred C. Kelly. 76 photographs. 96pp. 8¼ × 11. 25662-6 Pa. $8.95

THE ARTS OF THE SAILOR: Knotting, Splicing and Ropework, Hervey Garrett Smith. Indispensable shipboard reference covers tools, basic knots and useful hitches; handsewing and canvas work, more. Over 100 illustrations. Delightful reading for sea lovers. 256pp. 5⅜ × 8½. 26440-8 Pa. $7.95

FRANK LLOYD WRIGHT'S FALLINGWATER: The House and Its History, Second, Revised Edition, Donald Hoffmann. A total revision—both in text and illustrations—of the standard document on Fallingwater, the boldest, most personal architectural statement of Wright's mature years, updated with valuable new material from the recently opened Frank Lloyd Wright Archives. "Fascinating"—*The New York Times*. 116 illustrations. 128pp. 9¼ × 10¾. 27430-6 Pa. $10.95

PHOTOGRAPHIC SKETCHBOOK OF THE CIVIL WAR, Alexander Gardner. 100 photos taken on field during the Civil War. Famous shots of Manassas, Harper's Ferry, Lincoln, Richmond, slave pens, etc. 244pp. 10⅝ × 8¼.
22731-6 Pa. $9.95

FIVE ACRES AND INDEPENDENCE, Maurice G. Kains. Great back-to-the-land classic explains basics of self-sufficient farming. The one book to get. 95 illustrations. 397pp. 5⅜ × 8½. 20974-1 Pa. $7.95

SONGS OF EASTERN BIRDS, Dr. Donald J. Borror. Songs and calls of 60 species most common to eastern U.S.: warblers, woodpeckers, flycatchers, thrushes, larks, many more in high-quality recording. Cassette and manual 99912-2 $8.95

A MODERN HERBAL, Margaret Grieve. Much the fullest, most exact, most useful compilation of herbal material. Gigantic alphabetical encyclopedia, from aconite to zedoary, gives botanical information, medical properties, folklore, economic uses, much else. Indispensable to serious reader. 161 illustrations. 888pp. 6½ × 9¼. 2-vol. set. (USO) Vol. I: 22798-7 Pa. $9.95
Vol. II: 22799-5 Pa. $9.95

HIDDEN TREASURE MAZE BOOK, Dave Phillips. Solve 34 challenging mazes accompanied by heroic tales of adventure. Evil dragons, people-eating plants, bloodthirsty giants, many more dangerous adversaries lurk at every twist and turn. 34 mazes, stories, solutions. 48pp. 8¼ × 11. 24566-7 Pa. $2.95

LETTERS OF W. A. MOZART, Wolfgang A. Mozart. Remarkable letters show bawdy wit, humor, imagination, musical insights, contemporary musical world; includes some letters from Leopold Mozart. 276pp. 5⅜ × 8½. 22859-2 Pa. $7.95

BASIC PRINCIPLES OF CLASSICAL BALLET, Agrippina Vaganova. Great Russian theoretician, teacher explains methods for teaching classical ballet. 118 illustrations. 175pp. 5⅜ × 8½. 22036-2 Pa. $4.95

THE JUMPING FROG, Mark Twain. Revenge edition. The original story of The Celebrated Jumping Frog of Calaveras County, a hapless French translation, and Twain's hilarious "retranslation" from the French. 12 illustrations. 66pp. 5⅜ × 8½. 22686-7 Pa. $3.95

BEST REMEMBERED POEMS, Martin Gardner (ed.). The 126 poems in this superb collection of 19th- and 20th-century British and American verse range from Shelley's "To a Skylark" to the impassioned "Renascence" of Edna St. Vincent Millay and to Edward Lear's whimsical "The Owl and the Pussycat." 224pp. 5⅜ × 8½. 27165-X Pa. $4.95

COMPLETE SONNETS, William Shakespeare. Over 150 exquisite poems deal with love, friendship, the tyranny of time, beauty's evanescence, death and other themes in language of remarkable power, precision and beauty. Glossary of archaic terms. 80pp. 5³⁄₁₆ × 8¼. 26686-9 Pa. $1.00

BODIES IN A BOOKSHOP, R. T. Campbell. Challenging mystery of blackmail and murder with ingenious plot and superbly drawn characters. In the best tradition of British suspense fiction. 192pp. 5⅜ × 8½. 24720-1 Pa. $5.95

THE WIT AND HUMOR OF OSCAR WILDE, Alvin Redman (ed.). More than 1,000 ripostes, paradoxes, wisecracks: Work is the curse of the drinking classes; I can resist everything except temptation; etc. 258pp. 5⅜ × 8½. 20602-5 Pa. $5.95

SHAKESPEARE LEXICON AND QUOTATION DICTIONARY, Alexander Schmidt. Full definitions, locations, shades of meaning in every word in plays and poems. More than 50,000 exact quotations. 1,485pp. 6½ × 9¼. 2-vol. set.
Vol. I: 22726-X Pa. $16.95
Vol. 2: 22727-8 Pa. $15.95

SELECTED POEMS, Emily Dickinson. Over 100 best-known, best-loved poems by one of America's foremost poets, reprinted from authoritative early editions. No comparable edition at this price. Index of first lines. 64pp. 5³⁄₁₆ × 8¼.
26466-1 Pa. $1.00

CELEBRATED CASES OF JUDGE DEE (DEE GOONG AN), translated by Robert van Gulik. Authentic 18th-century Chinese detective novel; Dee and associates solve three interlocked cases. Led to van Gulik's own stories with same characters. Extensive introduction. 9 illustrations. 237pp. 5⅜ × 8½.
23337-5 Pa. $6.95

THE MALLEUS MALEFICARUM OF KRAMER AND SPRENGER, translated by Montague Summers. Full text of most important witchhunter's "bible," used by both Catholics and Protestants. 278pp. 6⅝ × 10. 22802-9 Pa. $11.95

SPANISH STORIES/CUENTOS ESPAÑOLES: A Dual-Language Book, Angel Flores (ed.). Unique format offers 13 great stories in Spanish by Cervantes, Borges, others. Faithful English translations on facing pages. 352pp. 5⅜ × 8½.
25399-6 Pa. $8.95

THE CHICAGO WORLD'S FAIR OF 1893: A Photographic Record, Stanley Appelbaum (ed.). 128 rare photos show 200 buildings, Beaux-Arts architecture, Midway, original Ferris Wheel, Edison's kinetoscope, more. Architectural emphasis; full text. 116pp. 8¼ × 11. 23990-X Pa. $9.95

OLD QUEENS, N.Y., IN EARLY PHOTOGRAPHS, Vincent F. Seyfried and William Asadorian. Over 160 rare photographs of Maspeth, Jamaica, Jackson Heights, and other areas. Vintage views of DeWitt Clinton mansion, 1939 World's Fair and more. Captions. 192pp. 8⅞ × 11. 26358-4 Pa. $12.95

CAPTURED BY THE INDIANS: 15 Firsthand Accounts, 1750-1870, Frederick Drimmer. Astounding true historical accounts of grisly torture, bloody conflicts, relentless pursuits, miraculous escapes and more, by people who lived to tell the tale. 384pp. 5⅜ × 8½. 24901-8 Pa. $8.95

THE WORLD'S GREAT SPEECHES, Lewis Copeland and Lawrence W. Lamm (eds.). Vast collection of 278 speeches of Greeks to 1970. Powerful and effective models; unique look at history. 842pp. 5⅜ × 8½. 20468-5 Pa. $14.95

THE BOOK OF THE SWORD, Sir Richard F. Burton. Great Victorian scholar/adventurer's eloquent, erudite history of the "queen of weapons"—from prehistory to early Roman Empire. Evolution and development of early swords, variations (sabre, broadsword, cutlass, scimitar, etc.), much more. 336pp. 6⅛ × 9¼. 25434-8 Pa. $8.95

AUTOBIOGRAPHY: The Story of My Experiments with Truth, Mohandas K. Gandhi. Boyhood, legal studies, purification, the growth of the Satyagraha (nonviolent protest) movement. Critical, inspiring work of the man responsible for the freedom of India. 480pp. 5⅜ × 8½. (USO) 24593-4 Pa. $8.95

CELTIC MYTHS AND LEGENDS, T. W. Rolleston. Masterful retelling of Irish and Welsh stories and tales. Cuchulain, King Arthur, Deirdre, the Grail, many more. First paperback edition. 58 full-page illustrations. 512pp. 5⅜ × 8½. 26507-2 Pa. $9.95

THE PRINCIPLES OF PSYCHOLOGY, William James. Famous long course complete, unabridged. Stream of thought, time perception, memory, experimental methods; great work decades ahead of its time. 94 figures. 1,391pp. 5⅜ × 8½. 2-vol. set.
Vol. I: 20381-6 Pa. $12.95
Vol. II: 20382-4 Pa. $12.95

THE WORLD AS WILL AND REPRESENTATION, Arthur Schopenhauer. Definitive English translation of Schopenhauer's life work, correcting more than 1,000 errors, omissions in earlier translations. Translated by E. F. J. Payne. Total of 1,269pp. 5⅜ × 8½. 2-vol. set.
Vol. 1: 21761-2 Pa. $11.95
Vol. 2: 21762-0 Pa. $11.95

MAGIC AND MYSTERY IN TIBET, Madame Alexandra David-Neel. Experiences among lamas, magicians, sages, sorcerers, Bonpa wizards. A true psychic discovery. 32 illustrations. 321pp. 5⅜ × 8½. (USO) 22682-4 Pa. $8.95

THE EGYPTIAN BOOK OF THE DEAD, E. A. Wallis Budge. Complete reproduction of Ani's papyrus, finest ever found. Full hieroglyphic text, interlinear transliteration, word-for-word translation, smooth translation. 533pp. 6½ × 9¼. 21866-X Pa. $9.95

MATHEMATICS FOR THE NONMATHEMATICIAN, Morris Kline. Detailed, college-level treatment of mathematics in cultural and historical context, with numerous exercises. Recommended Reading Lists. Tables. Numerous figures. 641pp. 5⅜ × 8½. 24823-2 Pa. $11.95

THEORY OF WING SECTIONS: Including a Summary of Airfoil Data, Ira H. Abbott and A. E. von Doenhoff. Concise compilation of subsonic aerodynamic characteristics of NACA wing sections, plus description of theory. 350pp. of tables. 693pp. 5⅜ × 8½. 60586-8 Pa. $14.95

THE RIME OF THE ANCIENT MARINER, Gustave Doré, S. T. Coleridge. Doré's finest work; 34 plates capture moods, subtleties of poem. Flawless full-size reproductions printed on facing pages with authoritative text of poem. "Beautiful. Simply beautiful."—*Publisher's Weekly*. 77pp. 9¼ × 12. 22305-1 Pa. $6.95

NORTH AMERICAN INDIAN DESIGNS FOR ARTISTS AND CRAFTSPEOPLE, Eva Wilson. Over 360 authentic copyright-free designs adapted from Navajo blankets, Hopi pottery, Sioux buffalo hides, more. Geometrics, symbolic figures, plant and animal motifs, etc. 128pp. 8⅜ × 11. (EUK) 25341-4 Pa. $7.95

SCULPTURE: Principles and Practice, Louis Slobodkin. Step-by-step approach to clay, plaster, metals, stone; classical and modern. 253 drawings, photos. 255pp. 8⅛ × 11. 22960-2 Pa. $10.95

CATALOG OF DOVER BOOKS

THE INFLUENCE OF SEA POWER UPON HISTORY, 1660–1783, A. T. Mahan. Influential classic of naval history and tactics still used as text in war colleges. First paperback edition. 4 maps. 24 battle plans. 640pp. 5⅜ × 8½.
25509-3 Pa. $12.95

THE STORY OF THE TITANIC AS TOLD BY ITS SURVIVORS, Jack Winocour (ed.). What it was really like. Panic, despair, shocking inefficiency, and a little heroism. More thrilling than any fictional account. 26 illustrations. 320pp. 5⅜ × 8½.
20610-6 Pa. $8.95

FAIRY AND FOLK TALES OF THE IRISH PEASANTRY, William Butler Yeats (ed.). Treasury of 64 tales from the twilight world of Celtic myth and legend: "The Soul Cages," "The Kildare Pooka," "King O'Toole and his Goose," many more. Introduction and Notes by W. B. Yeats. 352pp. 5⅜ × 8½.
26941-8 Pa. $8.95

BUDDHIST MAHAYANA TEXTS, E. B. Cowell and Others (eds.). Superb, accurate translations of basic documents in Mahayana Buddhism, highly important in history of religions. The Buddha-karita of Asvaghosha, Larger Sukhavativyuha, more. 448pp. 5⅜ × 8½. ,
25552-2 Pa. $9.95

ONE TWO THREE . . . INFINITY: Facts and Speculations of Science, George Gamow. Great physicist's fascinating, readable overview of contemporary science: number theory, relativity, fourth dimension, entropy, genes, atomic structure, much more. 128 illustrations. Index. 352pp. 5⅜ × 8½.
25664-2 Pa. $8.95

ENGINEERING IN HISTORY, Richard Shelton Kirby, et al. Broad, nontechnical survey of history's major technological advances: birth of Greek science, industrial revolution, electricity and applied science, 20th-century automation, much more. 181 illustrations. ". . . excellent . . ."—Isis. Bibliography. vii + 530pp. 5⅜ × 8¼.
26412-2 Pa. $14.95

Prices subject to change without notice.

Available at your book dealer or write for free catalog to Dept. GI, Dover Publications, Inc., 31 East 2nd St., Mineola, N.Y. 11501. Dover publishes more than 500 books each year on science, elementary and advanced mathematics, biology, music, art, literary history, social sciences and other areas.